Footnotes to

Philippine History

Footnotes to
Philippine
History

Renato Perdon

The Manila Prints
Sydney/Manila
2008

First published in 2008
by **The Manila Prints**
P. O. Box 1267
Darlinghurst NSW 2010, Australia
Tel. +61 2 9313 8179

and

Minor Prints
13 10th Street
Pacita Complex
San Pedro, Laguna, The Philippines
Tel. +63 2 8686513

National Library of Australia
Cataloguing-in-Publication entry

Perdon, Renato
Footnotes to Philippine History

1st ed.
ISBN 978-0-9804827-1-3 (pbk.)
Bibliography.
Filipinos.
Philippines–History.
Philippines–Civilization.
Philippines–Politics and government.
Philippines–Social life and customs.

959.9

Cover
Nicholas Chevalier (1828 - 1902)
Waiting for the Ferry, Manila 1881
oil on canvas, 126 x 75
Purchased with funds from the Morton Allport Bequest , 1972
AG2530, Collection: Tasmanian Museum and Art Gallery

The FLAG OF THE REVOLUTION. The three Ks stood for *Kataastaasang Kagalanggalang Katipunan* or " Most High and Most Sacred Society".

BONIFACIO'S FLAG. Made by women members of the Katipunan just before the revolution, this flag was first used at the Cry of Pugadlawin which took place on August 23, 1896. Seven days later, the same emblem was used in the Battle of Pinaglabanan in San Juan del Monte.

An EARLY VERSION of the KATIPUNAN FLAG has the three Ks arranged in an equivalent triangle.

MAGDIWANG FLAG. The Katipuneros of Cavite, particularly the Magdiwang chapter, used this flag. According to some historians, this was Aguinaldo's flag up to the time the Pack of Biyak-na-Bato was signed.

FLAG WITH ONLY ONE "K" AT THE CENTER. All versions had a red background to denote revolutionary character of the Katipunan.

FIRST OFFICIAL REVERSION. The first official revision of the flag took place after the 1897 Naic conference presided by Gen. Emilio Aguinaldo.

LLANERA'S FLAG. The flag used by Gen. Mariano Llanera in San Isidro, Nueva Ecija was sometimes called *Bungo ni Llanera* (Llanera's Skull). According to stories, Llanera derived his design from the Katipunan initiation rite using a black hat, white triangle and the letters Z, Ll, B.

GREGORIO DEL PILAR'S FLAG. This was the first among the Katipunan flags to use three colors: red, blue and black. According to del Pilar, the design was patterned after the flag of Cuba, then in revolt against Spain.

PIO DEL PILAR'S FLAG. Called *Bandila ng Magtagumpay* (Victorious Flag), this flag was first used on July 11, 1895 and stood witness to many battles. Pio del Pilar's flag carried eight rays in the rising sun to symbolize the first eight provinces' revolt.

THE PRESENT FLAG. The present flag has adapted features of all the previous Katipunan flags. It was waved in the balcony of Gen. Aguinaldo six weeks after the battle of Manila Bay. To set the standard size and colors, President Manuel L. Quezon issued an Executive Order on March 25, 1936.

Evolution of the Philippine Flag

Table of Contents

To the Filipino expatriates around the world and
their families who wish to re-enforce their
knowledge about Filipinos and the Philippines,
and hoping that this book will be a useful tool in
their interaction with people in foreign lands, this
humble work is sincerely dedicated

Foreword

One of the perils of public life is that you spend a lot of time cutting ribbons and delivering speeches. Higher office requires that you stand as principal sponsor in christenings and weddings. Sometimes government officials require a special fund for funeral wreaths. At the National Historical Institute the demands are different, there are many requests for messages in souvenir programs and forewords for books. I realized at one point that I was writing more forewords for other peoples books rather than my own so I started to avoid this task. Renato Perdon I could not refuse because I have known him for the past 25 years first as a young NHI division chief 25 years ago, now as an absentee landlord of a thriving pre-school and as a columnist for a Filipino newspaper in Australia.

Perdon was introduced to me by the eminent NHI board members: the historian Teodoro A. Agoncillo, and the late E. Aguilar Cruz, diplomat, journalist, and writer. We became fast friends and I would visit Perdon in his cubby hole in search of NHI publications and other historical materials. Perdon also showed me the cabinets filled with photos, artifacts, and even relics of our heroes that included Jose Rizal's clothing and a small clump of Apolinario Mabini's hair!

Through his friendship Perdon developed my interest in history. 25 years ago I read a magazine article of his regarding German Kaiser Wilhelm's plan to take the Philippines in 1898 and in retrospect I wished he spent more time writing because he had special access to obscure historical sources and a straightforward style that was much more pleasant than the constipated tone of academic historians.

When he left the Philippines to settle in Australia the country lost an able cultural administrator, but what is more important is the fact that he completed a graduate degree, and started to write regularly for a Filipino newspaper. They say that absence makes the heart grow fonder and this book is the fruit of a lifetime of research and interest in Philippine history. We hope there will be more to come.

Ambeth R. Ocampo
Chairman
National Historical Institute
The Philippines

Introduction

The idea for this present book germinated after the publication of my first history book entitled *Brown Americans of Asia* which was an expanded thesis for my academic degree in Master of Arts in Asian Studies from the University of New South Wales, Australia. Like any other book on history, some regarded it as largely distant and formidable, typical of serious books on history written by an academic or written as a textbook aiming at classroom use. During the promotion of the book, I learned from many Filipino expatriates in Australia and those in other countries that the type of books they want are something from which they can get ready information about Philippine history and culture to answer urgent questions that surfaced in their interaction with people in their new environment overseas. Time is of the essence. They don't have time to sit down and read book length historical writings aimed at readers who have the luxury of time on their hands. In simple words, what is needed are non-academic books on Philippine history that anyone of the eight million Global Filipinos scattered throughout the world would easily use as a back-up reference to what they already know about the Philippines, not a history book with dogmatic and largely unimaginative academic approaches to Philippine history.

What came to mind, therefore, were historical writings produced by historian-journalists and not by professional historians. These are the likes produced by Raul Ingles who popularized his column *Fifty Years Ago*, Carmen Guerrero Nakpil for her *History Today* and *Consensus of One*, Pura Santillan-Castrence for her *As I See It*, Miguel Bernad for his *At*

Random newspaper column, and the works of Doreen Fernandez, E. Aguilar Cruz, and the great Nick Joaquin who made reading history as a jovial experience and not a burden. This kind of writing called 'history in a hurry' is currently popular because of the prolific and imaginative style of historical writings like those of Ambeth Ocampo, regarded as the country's 'pop historian'. Ocampo is known for his newspaper column in *The Philippine Daily Inquirer* called *Looking Back,* which has been compiled into a number of books that have become best sellers because of his style and the substance of the writing itself. Academic historian Vicente Rafael advanced the reason behind the popularity of this kind of historical writing as mainly due to its 'conciseness and portability designed for quick perusal and daily disposal.' This is probably the reason why the late Pura Santillan-Castrence admitted that 'Filipinos, although they care for education, generally do not love books. They read up on materials relating to their specific field of study, but eschew everything else.'

Many Filipinos regard academic history as a serious topic because of dogmas and definitive treatises used by historians. Many are turned off engaging in history reading, because it is regarded as not only boring, but a waste of time in this age of globalization.

This volume, which is a compilation of selected historical essays published originally in the *Bayanihan News*, a Filipino community newspaper in Australia, is therefore not an attempt to produce great historical writings in the tradition of the popular pieces produced by historian-journalists mentioned above, but it is envisioned to capture the kind of information that Global Filipinos need in their current situation – to serve as a quick reference for the information they need mostly during their interaction with other people in foreign lands, whether they are in Australia, Europe, the United States, the Middle East or Asia and the Pacific.

The essays have been grouped into three parts, with the first providing answers to the question of Filipino identity, and how that identity formed. What are the symbols of Filipino identity, national and political? Then it moves to the second part to discuss why Filipinos became known as 'brown Americans of Asia', and explain how the Americans changed the lives of Filipinos with their Pacific adventure, and how the Americanization of the Filipinos was realized easily. The last part talks about Global Filipinos and how they survive outside the Philippines and the problems they encounter. How does Filipino migration help the Philippines survive? Discussion also follows about two issues needing clarification – the Philippines' territorial claims on Sabah and the Spratlys, and, finally, revisiting the life of Imelda R. Marcos, the most maligned woman in Philippine history and how she is compared to another controversial figure in another country's history – Evita Peron, the former First Lady of Argentina.

It is hoped that this book will provide ready answers to questions asked of Filipino expatriates throughout the world about them and the Philippines. Also, it is hoped that interest would be generated from reading these essays to encourage further reading during their spare time.

– The author

Acknowledgment

Acknowledgment must be made to the many people who in one way or the other contributed to provoke my interest in this task – writing a book that will be useful to many Filipino expatriates throughout the world.

To the libraries, archives and other cultural institutions in Australia and in the Philippines, and to their staff: the National Historical Institute, the National Library of the Philippines, the Cultural Centre of the Philippines, the National Archives of the Philippines, the Fisher Library (Sydney University), the UNSW Library, the Australian Archives, the Torres Strait Historical Association, the Queensland State Archives, and, in particular, the Historical Data Bank of the National Historical Institute of the Philippines, the *Bayanihan News* for permission to use the articles which were orginally published in the said Filipino community newspaper, to language specialist Aila Edgarda Lenard and historian Dr. Samuel K. Tan for feedback and reading the final manuscript, and to the Tasmanian Museum and Art Gallery for permission to use an image of Nicholas Chevalier's *Waiting for the Ferry, Manila 1881* from its collection for this book I am deeply grateful. Also, much appreciation to Ambeth R. Ocampo, Chairman, National Historical Institute, for writing a foreword. And lastly, Dr. Paul W. Mathews' skilful editing of the tyspescript is much appreciated. And to the others I may have missed, my apology.

Errors and mistakes that might be found in this work are solely the responsibility of the author, no one else.

– The author

The Making of
Filipino Identity

1

Filipinos and the Philippines

More than a hundred years ago, the Filipinos took arms against the Spanish colonial authorities. The main objective was to end colonialism and start a new life as independent people.

The event that had taken place in the Philippines forever changed the course of history, not only for the country, but for Asia as well. Within four years, the *Katipunan*, the secret society founded by Andres Bonifacio in 1892 and whose main purpose was to overthrow the Spanish colonial government, had increased in membership, many of whom became impatient at the slow progress in the struggle. Many were waiting for the glorious moment, the day to strike against the oppressors.

In fact, nightly meetings were held and this generated suspicions among the Spanish authorities. Situations became tense when rumours were widely circulating that arms and ammunition landed in the Philippines from Hong Kong and Japan. Church officials, particularly the priests, capitalized on the situation and tried to influence the Spanish colonial authorities to act. They took upon themselves to act as the eyes and ears of the colonial authorities. The church authorities even encouraged the spread of rumours among the population in their efforts to extract the needed information about the secret society from their Filipino servants, but the government was adamant against reacting right away on unverified rumours.

Meanwhile, two members of the Katipunan, Apolonio de la Cruz and Teodoro Patiño, workers at the *Diario de Manila* Printing press, had a personal disagreement and the irritants led to the discovery of the *Katipunan*. Patiño told his sister, who was staying at the orphanage managed by religious nuns, about the secret society. His sister, shocked by the revelation, told the nuns about what her brother just told her. It was suggested that Patiño should talk to Father Mariano Gil, the parish priest of Tondo, and tell the homely about the whole story.

On 19 August, the priest learned from Patiño the existence of the *Katipunan* and immediately he acted. The priest went to the printing press and found the printing paraphernalia used by the *Katipunan* in printing its propaganda materials. More evidence was found and eventually turned over to the police. The events that followed were swift. Mass arrests of Filipinos suspected of being members of the *Katipunan* were made and they were placed behind bars. More than 500 persons were initially arrested and convicted of illegal association and thrown into Fort Santiago, in Intramuros.

The news of the discovery of the *Katipunan* reached the officers of the society. Andres Bonifacio called for an emergency meeting of officials to decide on the next move. Since the Spanish authorities, by that time, started to clamp down on the members of the society, the situation was tense. Before the end of the third day, many rebels left Balintawak and proceeded to Kangkong. By 22 August they arrived at the house of Juan Ramos in Pugadlawin where they rested and were served hot meals by the host.

It was at this stage that Bonifacio decided to ask all those present, around 500 of them, whether they were prepared to fight to the last. Everyone agreed. The *Katipunan* supremo then asked everyone to bring out their *cedulas* (identification document) and asked the members to destroy them as a symbol of their defiance of the Spanish authorities. Everyone did what was asked of them, and while they were tearing their cedulas, they were shouting 'Long Live the Philippines.' This was the *Cry of Pugadlawin* that took place on 23 August 1896.

Meanwhile, more *Katipuneros* arrived and brought the news that they were being pursued by the Spanish civil guards. Due to lack of arms that could start a fight against the enemy, the *Katipuneros* decided to retreat, and marched towards Pasong Tamo. On 24 August they arrived at the house of Melchora Aquino, popularly known among *Katipuneros* as Tandang Sora.

The general attack on Manila was decided to be made on the night of 29 August. A manifesto addressed to Filipinos asking them to rise up was issued by Bonifacio. It said:

'This manifesto is for all of you. It is absolutely necessary for us to stop at the earliest possible time the nameless oppressions being perpetrated on the sons of the people who are now suffering the brutal punishment and tortures in jails, and because of this please let all the brethren know that on Saturday, the revolution shall commence according to our agreement.'

The first bloody encounter took place in San Juan del Monte on 30 August 1896. The main target was to seize the Spanish powder storage. However, with untrained and poorly armed supporters, whose main weapons were crude *bolos* and few firearms and a strong belief in *anting-anting*, the Filipinos, although fighting bravely and courageously, lost the battle. Many of them were slaughtered by the Spanish troops with their deadly volleys of rifle and artillery shots.

John Foreman, a British trader who was residing in Manila at the time of the Battle of Pinaglabanan or San Juan del Monte, described the incident:

'About 4 a.m. on Sunday, August 30, the rebels concentrated in the village of San Juan del Monte, distant half an hour on horseback from the city gates. They endeavoured to seize the powder magazine. One Spanish artilleryman was killed and several of the defenders were badly wounded whilst engaged in dropping ammunition from window openings into a stream which runs close by.

'Cavalry and infantry re-enforcements were at once sent out, and the first battle was fought at the entrance to the village of San Juan del Monte. The rebels made a hard stand this time under the leadership of Sancho Valenzuela (a hemp-rope maker in a fairly good way of business), but he showed no military skills and childly directed his men by frantic shouts from the window of a wooden house. Naturally, as soon as they had to retreat, Valenzuela and his three companions were taken prisoners. 'The rebels left about 153 dead on the field and fled towards the Pasig River which they tried to cross. Their passage was at first cut-off by gunboats, which fired volleys into the retreating mob and drove them higher up the bank, where there was some hand-to-hand fighting. Over a hundred managed to get into canoes with the hope of reaching the Lake of Bay; but as they passed up the river the civil guards, waiting in ambush on the opposite shore, fired upon them, and in the consequent confusion every canoe was upset. The loss to the rebels in the river and on the bank was reckoned at about 50. The whole of that day the road to San Juan del Monte was occupied by troops, and no civilian was allowed to pass. At 3 p.m. the same day martial law was proclaimed in Manila and seven other Luzon provinces.

'The next morning at sunrise, I rode out to the battlefield with the correspondent of the *Ejercito Español* (Madrid). The rebels slain had not yet been removed. We came across them everywhere – in the fields and in the gutters of the highroad.

'Old men and youths had joined the scrimmage and, with one exception, every corpse we saw was attired in the usual working dress. This one exception we found literally upside down with his head stuck in the mud of a paddy-field. Our attention was drawn to him (and possibly, the Spaniards' bullets, too) by his bright red baggy suave trousers. We rode to the village, which was at the estate house of the friars where the Spanish officers lodged. The padre looked extremely anxious, and the officers advised us not to take the road we intended, as rebel parties were known to be lurking there. The military advice being practically a command, we took the highroad to Sampaloc on our way back to the city.'

4

The origin of Filipino

The word *Filipino*, as we understand it today, is just a 100 years old. The inhabitants of the Philippines were not officially known as *Filipinos* until the late 19th century. In 1521, the Portuguese navigator Ferdinand Magellan 'discovered' the Philippine Islands for the Western world and called the early inhabitants *indios*, meaning the indigenous, autochthonous aboriginal or native inhabitants of the islands. Magellan's act followed the common practice by Spain of calling the original inhabitants of the lands 'discovered' and colonized by the Spanish *conquistadores*, regardless of their location in the world, as *indios*.

In 1543, Bernardo de la Torre, a member of the Villalobos Expedition named the Samar-Leyte region in the Visayas as *Felipinas*, in honour of then Prince Philip of Asturias, who later became Philip II of Spain. In 1565, the name became *Las Filipinas*, thanks to Adelantado Miguel Lopez de Legaspi who applied the name to the entire archipelago. The official name given to the islands, however, did not alter the name given to its early inhabitants by Magellan. The name *indio* remained and had an added connotation of inferior, therefore, primitive.

During the entire Spanish domination of the islands, the Philippines' social structure consisted of five layers, namely: the Spanish-born residents known as *peninsulares*; the full-blooded Spaniards born in the Philippines called either *filipinos* or *insulares*; the Spanish mixed-breeds called *mestizo*; the Chinese *mestizo*; and the *indios*, the indigenous inhabitants. Among these groups a hidden distinction of superior and inferior races existed. The mutual antipathy between the first two social classes was real, although well disguised. The first considered the latter as 'inferior' to them and less intellectually endowed. The *mestizo*, a product of racial intermarriage, was not recognized as a separate

5

legal group. In fact, they were classed among the 'colored' population by the *peninsulares*. The Spaniards, the *filipino*, and the *insulares* looked down upon the *mestizos* who, in turn, looked down upon the *indios*. As a result, the first three classes in the social ladder, who acted in the same manner when dealing with the *indios,* were despised and hated by the full-blooded inhabitants who, in retaliation, called the non-indios *kastila*, a pejorative name.

In spite of the growing number of the *indio* population who did not distinguish between *peninsulares* and *filipinos*, this social structure continued until the middle of the 19th century. As far as the natives were concerned, the privileged white population of the Philippines was all the *kastila*. The *indios*, the *peninsulares* and the *filipinos* or *insulares*, not to mention the *mestizos*, both the Spanish and the Chinese-mixed bloods, did co-exist in the islands. Taken as a group, the Spaniards, who comprised the first two classes, represented a smaller percentage of the population. Most of them belonged either to the Church or to the State. The census of 1883 indicated that 95 per cent of the population of the Philippines was *indios,* while 4 per cent comprised the *mestizos* (European and Chinese). Only 1 percent of the population was Spanish and those of Spanish descent. The number of people called *filipinos* was never large, as there was only just over 1,000 male adult Filipinos during that period.

The opening of Philippine ports to foreign trade and the introduction of European liberal ideas resulted in the emergence of a middle class during the early 1800s. This brought changes in the interaction between the inhabitants. The middle class, comprised mainly by the *mestizos*, started to think of themselves as *Filipinos*, the same definition of the word as we know it today, and they no longer aspired to become Spaniards in the

Philippines. *Mestizos* were relaxing about being regarded as natives of the islands. The first Filipino patriotic sentiment may be dated to the 1860s when Fr. Jose Burgos, a talented Spanish–Filipino *mestizo* who fought for the interests of Filipino priests, wrote a *Manifesto addressed by the loyal Filipinos to the noble Spanish Nation* which clearly identified the inhabitants as *Filipinos*, not as full-blooded Spaniards born in the Philippines. This was a new meaning applied to an old name. Fr. Burgos used the term to refer to a new group in the colony, a group comprised of not just the natives, but also the Chinese *mestizos*, Spanish *mestizos*, and the full-blooded Spaniards born in the Philippines, as well.

The new meaning of the term *Filipino* began to enter the common usage and consciousness of the people, at least in patriotic and reform literature. But it was not a universal usage for the Spanish friars and *peninsulares* who insisted on naming the different sub-groups separately and continued to call the natives *indios* until the end of the Spanish regime. In 1879, Jose Rizal, then a young student at the University of Santo Tomas, wrote a poem entitled *A La Juventud Filipina* (To the Filipino Youth). Rallying the Filipino youth whom he considered the 'hope of the fatherland', Rizal urged them to develop their talents for their native land – the Philippines. He no longer referred to Spain as the 'mother country'.

Filipino, as an official symbol of identity in the present context, was not achieved until April 1898 when the Spanish–American War broke out. Spanish Governor-General Basilio Augustin issued a proclamation calling for the loyalty and support of the *indios* against the US troops. He asked the population not as *indios* but as '*Filipinos* ... let us fight with the conviction that victory will reward our efforts against the shouts of our enemies, let us resist with Christian decision and the patriotic cry of *viva España*', he said.

With the expulsion of the Spaniards, the archipelago passed briefly into the hands of the natives. The term *filipino* clearly could no longer mean what it was during the Spanish period — a 'full-blooded Spaniard born in the Philippines'. It now referred to the indigenous population of the Philippines, previously called *indios*. The use of the term *filipino* to identify the Malay population caused no confusion among the *indios*, for under Spanish rule the term was not ambiguous to them at all. They did not care about the artificial distinction which the Spaniards maintained between those born in Spain and the Spaniards born in the Philippines. The above highlights the difference between the *filipino* of the Spanish period and the *Filipino* of today.

It is interesting to note that Andres Bonifacio, the great plebeian and leader of the *Katipunan*, did not refer to the inhabitants of the Philippines as *Filipinos*. In his writings, *Katapusang Hibik ng Pilipinas* and *Pag-Ibig sa Tinubuang Lupa*, Bonifacio called the inhabitants Tagalogs and the Philippine Islands as *katagalugan* (Tagalog region).

This illustrates how the Filipinos themselves regarded the name. Not everyone is serious about the name *Filipino*. Some sectors of society have been clamoring to change the name because they believe that King Philip II from whom the Filipinos were named does not deserve commemoration and that the name *Filipinas* has no historical or social justification. In 1995, a member of the Philippine Congress introduced a bill changing the name of the Filipinos to Filipinians to further strengthen the country's link with the neighboring Indonesians, Malaysians and the Singaporeans. According to the distinguished member of the Philippine lawmaking body who introduced the bill, the change was needed to counteract the negative image of Filipinos, who are associated with domestic helpers, entertainers, contract workers, and the caricature of the 'mail-order' brides. The *Times Journal*, a national newspaper in the Philippines, came up with a light hearted rejoinder and proposed the name Filipinese in the same manner that the Taiwanese, the Japanese and the Chinese are called.

A few years back, in 1967, there was a proposal to change the name of the Philippines to *Rizalia*, thereby calling its inhabitants as Rizalians. Other proposed names for the Philippines include *Tagalia, Luzviminda* (Luzon-Visayas-Mindanao*)*, *Luviminda, Silangan* (East), *Katagalogan* (Tagalog region*)*, and *Maharlika* (noble). Whatever the arguments against or in favor of changing the name Filipino, it is worth remembering what the late Filipino historian, Domingo Abella, said on the subject. He stated that Filipino as an identifier of the Philippines is 'one of the greatest achievements of the Malay Filipinos: the laborious process by which, surmounting racial prejudice and institutionalized discrimination, the Malays transformed themselves from the lowly *indio*, a colonial subject, to the independent *Filipino* of today.'

Filipino names

One of the cultural symbols that easily distinguishes a migrant from another in Australia, or that matter throughout the world, is his or her surname. This is particularly true of Asians who are socially visible because of their racial and cultural distinctiveness and whose names reveal their country of origin. It would be next to impossible not to know that the Nguyens are Vietnamese; the Hoonsakulas are Thais; the Sanagaras are Indonesians; the Sauthorns are Laotians; the Lees are Singaporeans or Chinese; the Yamadas are Japanese; and the Mauangs are Burmese.

Indeed, these names are distinctively Oriental in sound and in written form. For Filipinos, whose colonial experience had made them unique in Asia, however, their names, as a form of ethnic identification, contradict Australian perceptions of Asian iden-

9

tification – that of people coming from the Orient. Many Australians have noted that the names of their Filipino friends and acquaintances do not show their Oriental origin. Filipinos, more often than not, are introduced as Jose Maria Silos, Josefa Prudente, Celia Buenaventura, Manuel Castillo, Lino Bautista, Purisima Tuazon and other common names more popularly known in South American countries. In fact, in the US until the early 1970s, Filipinos were grouped demographically not as Asians but as part of the 'Spanish-speaking minority', in the company of Puerto Ricans, Cubans, Mexicans, and other nationals of South America. The names of Filipino heroes have followed the same pattern: Rafael Palma, Juan Luna, Gregorio del Pilar, Andres Bonifacio, Benigno Aquino and Emilio Aguinaldo. Even the name of former Philippine Presidents Fidel V. Ramos and Corazon C Aquino are not of native origin. They are Spanish translation of the English words *branch of a tree* and *heart*, respectively.

The colonial belief that the Philippines were part, first, of Spain, then, of the US, lives on owing mainly to their surnames which date back to a decree called *Catálogo Alfabético de Appellidos* (Alphabetised Catalogue of Surnames) issued by the Spanish Governor-General Narciso Claveria on 21 November 1849. Recalling this confusion more than three decades later, Jose Rizal wrote to his Austrian friend Ferdinand Blumentritt, 'I am the only Rizal because at home my parents, my sisters, my brother and my relatives have always preferred our old surname, Mercado.' Rizal told Blumentritt that his family name was indeed Mercado, but there were many Mercados in the Philippines who were not related to them. It was a provincial governor, a friend of the family, who added Rizal to his name.

Governor Claveria arrived in the Philippines in July 1844 to take up his post as head of the Spanish colonial government.

Archival sources indicate that Claveria was not the typical King's representative sent to the Spanish colonies. Before him, the official colonial preoccupation, upon arrival in their new post, was to enrich themselves at the expense of the natives. Claveria carried out the duties of the new colonial administrator with clean hands and brought changes to the islands. He was credited for introducing the election of town mayors and other local officials. He ordered local boundary changes, corrected the Philippine calendar (which for more than 300 years was one day behind that of the rest of Asia) and, most importantly, ordered the adoption of surnames for Filipinos in 1849.

It was during Claveria's countless visits to the country that he realised that the Filipinos, in general, were not using surnames to distinguish themselves by families. Filipinos capriciously adopted the names of saints, and this resulted in the existence of thousands of individuals having the same surnames, although unrelated. He also experienced the confusion that hindered the implementation of regulations governing the administration of justice, public service, finance and public order. Claveria noted too, that the moral, civil and religious implications of family names were not being transmitted from the parents to their children. He realized that, because of the situation, it became impossible to prove the degree of blood relations between parties to a marriage.

A catalogue of family names was therefore compiled, incorporating both Spanish surnames and native names earlier collected by the religious orders. The catalogue also adopted names from the vegetable and mineral kingdoms, geography, arts, and others. Surnames such as *Lopez, Santos, Fontanilla, Garcia, Dedal, Mella, Montejo, Sarmiento,* and *Sarte* became part of the list. Some native words included in the list were *bigas* (rice), *bigla* (quick), *batungbacal* (metal stone) *apdo* (bile), *limot* (forget), *maiz* (corn), and *bubuyog* (bumblebee). The selection of words was not strictly supervised and this resulted in some embarrassing surnames adopted by the Filipinos such as *utang* (debt), *teta* (nipple), *temblor* (earthquake), *mesa* (table), *moneda* (money), and *duling* (cross-eyed).

The reason behind issuing the decree was the need to establish a civil register that would be the basis for Philippine statistics. Aside from record-taking, the register was also aimed at exacting information on population movements, control of illegal migrants, tax evasion, personal service or forced labour avoidance, and other abuses resulting from the lack of any effective way of identifying the inhabitants. Claveria's decree ordered Filipino families to adopt surnames from a printed alphabetical list. Pages from this catalogue were sent to all provincial governors who distributed them to the mayors of various towns. Every town, in accordance with the number of families within its jurisdiction, was assigned a number of surnames arranged according to letters. The distribution was undertaken through the parish priests in every *barrio* or village community, with the help of the town mayor, another municipal official and two competent members of the community. The father or the oldest person of each family was assigned a surname from the list that was then adopted as the point of identification for the family and his direct descendants. Also, it was that person's responsibility to inform other members of the family not residing with him or her about the new surname assigned to the family.

Spanish residents, Filipinos and Chinese who already had surnames were allowed to retain theirs and were authorised to pass them on to their descendants. On the other hand, orphans were given the surnames of their paternal grandparents, but if this was not feasible, they were allowed to adopt the surname of the brothers or relatives of their natural father, ensuring that those coming from the same family branch had the same surnames.

Illegitimate offspring were given the surname of their mother or the surname of their guardian or their godfather. This was a common practice, principally, among the Chinese who were converted to Christianity. In some cases the name of the parish priest was allowed to be used. Surnames previously authorised by the King such as *Mojica*, *Tupas*, and *Raha Matanda*, were allowed to continue so that those affected would not be denied the privileges and status guaranteed by the Spanish monarch. This was particularly true among pre-colonial names of chiefs like *Sula* and *Lapulapu* of Mactan, *Lakandula* of Manila, *Raha Kolambu* of Butuan, and *Raha Sulayman* of Tondo. Families who had adopted the names of saints as their surnames for 40 years (since 1809) were allowed to pass their surnames on to their descendants with special permission from parish priests or provincial governors.

Historians have observed that the whole exercise of assigning new names to the Filipinos was undertaken democratically, an unusual procedure at that time. Each *barrio* was given two or three days to submit objections to the assigned surnames before the parish priest, who, guided by the provisions of the Claveria decree, acted on these objections. The decree was strictly enforced. Teachers were compelled to keep a register of all their pupils, listing their first names and surnames in that order. They were forbidden to address a student except by the assigned surnames. Non-compliance with this instruction was considered an offence and punishment decided by the leader of the provincial government. Even the military did not escape from this decree. The town mayor and the respective heads of *barrios*, with the concurrence of the parish priest, furnished the head of the provincial government with a list of surnames of soldiers. These surnames were then checked to find out whether they corresponded to each soldier's personal file.

At baptism, the parish priest required, in addition to the name to be given to the one to be baptized, the names and surnames of the person's father and mother, except in cases of illegitimate children. The same was required in the solemnization of marriage. All church and official documents required the surnames of parties to whom the documents would be issued. These documents were certified by the master registers, otherwise the documents were not deemed valid. This procedure was observed in capital cities, municipal and provincial courts, by authorities, military chiefs of the navy, treasury and other officials. Any person who changed his or her assigned name or surname was penalized and given a minimum penalty of eight days in jail or a three peso fine.

In spite of the rigidity of implementing the decree, accidents happened. In some places, only a few pages of the catalogue arrived. This is the reason why, even today, in many towns of the Philippines, there are people whose surnames almost all begin with the letter *A*, another with *B*, and so on. Another reason was that in some provinces the catalogue was fanned out starting with the letter *A* at the capital and the following letters *B* to *Z* were distributed to the outlying areas until the whole province was saturated with pages from the catalogue.

To illustrate, in the Bicol town of Oas, Albay, a province located south of Manila, almost all the inhabitants have surnames beginning with the letter *R* such as Reburriano, Roa, Reodica, Ralto, Robido, and so on. By knowing the surnames some observant Filipinos could identify which area in the Philippines a person came from. If the same decree were issued in Australia, it would have a catastrophic result, particularly for genealogists. Without knowing both the old and the new surnames, it would be impossible to record a Filipino family tree before 1849. No one has undertaken a historical study on the effect of this decree on the Filipinos. One thing is sure, however, the Filipinos, wherever they are, and whether they like it or not, will go on living with the consequences of this historical accident. To Filipino–Australians, a change of surname, if female, on marriage to an Australian with an Anglo–Celtic surname is an option. Others can change their names by deed poll.

Filipino Traits

Filipino traits are basically Malayan and characterize the Filipinos as a people. These traits are the result of succession and the mingling of waves of cultural influences, and they are recognized today as basic in the Filipino Family. Some of the common traits of Filipinos that are clearly evident are their hospitality, close family ties, fatalistic attitude, and loyalty. Sensitiveness, lack of initiative, curiosity and jealousy could also be regarded as national traits.

Hospitality – Filipino hospitality has been known the world over and it is this particular trait that immediately appeals to foreigners. According to the late historian Teodoro A. Agoncillo, Filipino hospitality is 'something that is almost to a fault.'

Hospitality is a strong point in the native character. Filipinos normally would exert enough effort to insure that life is worth living for their visitors. In extending hospitality, Filipinos will spare nothing from the basket or store or garden or house accommodation in their effort to make the visitor feel perfectly welcome to all that the homes afforded. Hospitality is evident in our very language. To a visitor, whoever he/she may be, the host or hostess is generally heard to say 'my house is small and the things I can offer you are poor, but the heart is large.' And it has been proven that the Filipino opens not only the door of his/her house, but also the door of his/her heart.

To illustrate further, Agoncillo observed that if you are a stranger and you have lost your way, knock at the door of even the humblest nipa hut and the occupant offers you his/her home. They open their heart, even to a complete stranger, and offers the visitor the best in his/her kitchen and bed chamber. Some call this trait as a sign of inferiority and the tendency to become submissive, particularly to white foreigners. But this has been disputed. Writing in 1787, a Frenchman said that the Filipinos 'seem no way inferior to those of Europe. I have gone through their villages and I have found them kind, hospitable, and affable.' In one of the letters to the editor received in 1966 by the now defunct *The Manila Times*, a certain S. Goddard observed that the traits (hospitality among them) of Filipinos are wholly positive, even if they do not represent the whole of the Filipino character. Jagor, the famous European traveler, said in his *Travel in the Philippines,* that 'Filipino hospitality is ample and much more comprehensive than that practice in Europe.'

One of the outstanding expressions of this hospitality is the town fiesta. It is its supreme characteristic. For example, when a visitor is invited to eat, they (hosts or hostesses) are not contented by merely calling out his name. The good hearted hosts will go to the extent of taking the visitor from his/her seat and conduct him/her to the table to eat. During the early American period, one American writer observed that 'strangers of all classes find in these (Filipino) villages a hospitality so invariable that hotels rarely exist except in the cities and a few of the largest towns.

Close Family Ties – the Filipinos, no doubt, have very close family ties. During the early times, historical facts prove that a strong relationships among the early inhabitants were safeguarded and exalted. And this is best illustrated by the fact that the Filipino family has been the unit of society and everything revolves around it. The Filipino family structural set-up is made of grandparents, parents, children and other relatives. The father is the head of the family while the mother is usually the business manager of the household, keeps the keys, does the providing, and receives all cash earned by any member of the family. In some cases, aged and other dependent relatives are welcome members of the household. It is therefore rare to see a homeless aged or crippled person. This is one of the reasons why an average Filipino family is a big one compared to other countries. The family extends to three generations in the direct line and more often than not includes the brothers and sisters and their spouses and children. It is governed by the principle of kinship and recognizes even distant relatives.

The best illustration of Filipino close family ties is the so-called *compadre* system. In Alemar's *Sociology in the Philippine Setting*, this is vividly described as: 'the size of the family is not dependent altogether on the birth rate but is extended by the *compadre* system. The *compadre* or *comadre* becomes known to the child as *Ninong* or *Ninang* and their children are *kapatid sa binyag* to the baptized child. This means that through the religious rite of baptism the *compadre* becomes somewhat of a brother to the parents of the child, and assumes a modified type of parental relationship to the child, while the *kapatid sa binyag* move into somewhat of a fraternal relationship to the child. The *compadre* relationship extends the line of family beyond that set even by broad consanguinal lines, and throughout life one has certain privileges and responsibilities to those with whom he is connected by the ties of the *compadre* system.'

Among the Badjao people in the southern Philippines, the family unit may consist of a married man and his several married sons or daughters, or a married man *and* his several married sons and daughters.

17

Fatalistic attitude – Fatalism in Filipinos is best illustrated by their *bahala na* mentality. A *bahala na* attitude is already ingrained in the Filipino social system. In everyday life and in almost all undertakings, we say *bahala na*. When we are not sure of our action we utter the same words. Fatalism, as Agoncillo stated, has bred in the Filipino a sense of resignation. Because of this, he/she faces disaster or tragedy with resignation. But this *bahala na* is considered a blessing in disguise, for it prevents the Filipino from being a crackpot.

Loyalty – Loyalty among Filipinos is very strong. Loyalty is characterized by a strong sense of *hiya* and *utang na loob*, or a debt of gratitude. When a person extends a helping hand, no matter how insignificant it is, the receiver will remember it to the end of his/her days. The essence of *utang na loob*, therefore, is interpreted as the imposition of an obligation of gratitude which the individual may never be able to repay.

Discussing the subject of *utang na loob*, Mary Hollinsteiner, a noted authority on Philippine sociology, said that 'every Filipino is expected to possess *utang na loob*: that is, he should be aware of his obligations to those from whom he receives favors and should repay them in an acceptable manner... failure to make payment through gifts or services indicating recognition of the debt causes or should cause *hiya*.

Religion and Filipinos

The Philippines has been considered different from its Asian neighbours because of two distinct Western cultural imports — Christianity from Spain, and a republican democracy and free enterprise from the US. This observation holds true today for the thirteenth largest nation in the world in terms of population – more than 80 million. The Philippines is noted for its almost universal acceptance of Christianity and the Western democratic institutions that dominate, govern and control its everyday life. This is probably the reason behind a popular statement that describes Filipinos as 'people who spent three hundred and fifty years in a religious monastery, then fifty years in a Hollywood-style campus'. One imagines a person who has been suppressed, all his/her life, in so many ways being suddenly confronted by a situation such as a Hollywood lifestyle. Indeed, three centuries of Catholic tradition and ecclesiastical teaching have had a profound influence on the Filipinos and its strong hold continues to dominate their contemporary consciousness.

A significant proportion of the population of 80 million belongs to the Roman Catholic Church. It is very rare to find a prominent Filipino who was not at least baptized a Roman Catholic. The ordinary Filipino is loyal to the church and takes pride, particularly if they are an overseas resident, in being from the only Christian nation in all Asia. This strong affinity for religion is not surprising, for Roman Catholics predominate in the Philippines, constituting about 83 per cent of the population. Protestants follow with 9 per cent and Muslims 5 per cent. Other religions which constitute the remaining 3 per cent include other denominations such as the Church of Christ (Iglesia ni Kristo, a Philippine sect), the Convention of Philippine Baptist Churches, the Lutherans, the Philippine Independent Church (Aglipayan Church, another Philippine sect), the Union Church of Manila and the United Church of Christ. A small Buddhist community exists, while animist beliefs are still practiced in remote areas.

It has been claimed that Filipino Christianity is different from the mindset that is found in the Western world where it originated. Some observers consider that the religious beliefs of the Filipinos border on fanaticism and extremism. To better understand the religious perspective of the Filipinos, we need to look at the religious belief system before the Spanish arrival. It was the attributes of the old religious belief that provided the foundation and give a clearer picture of Christianity as practiced in the Philippines today.

The primitive or pre-Spanish religion of the Filipinos was *animism*, a kind of ancestor worship. In spite of the absence of temples as symbols of divinity, there is evidence to show that there was a system of belief in signs and omens, and in a world that was populated by spirits of exotic animals. There were spirits resident in hills, trees, and other features of the natural environment, and personified forces in lightning and thunder. There were gods that favored success or failure in the harvest, in the hunt, in personal undertakings such as marriage, and in community enterprises such as tribal wars. There was a high regard for a Supreme Being known as *Bathala*. Ancient Filipinos also believed in the life beyond. According to Dr. Robert Fox, an authority on Philippine anthropology and archaeology, the principal ritual practices of the pre-Spanish Filipinos were based upon 'beliefs in environmental-spirits, soul-spirits, and a hierarchy of deities led by a ranking deity, not a supreme deity, for each had specific and some independent functions.' In her study of the ancient beliefs of the people of Pangasinan, for instance, Rosario Mendoza Cortes found similarities in their religious beliefs that confirm what Dr. Fox described. The *amagaoley*, according to Cortes, was the highest deity to whom the people prayed before they embarked on a voyage, a journey or any business. The *anitos* were environmental-spirits which were either good or bad. To the bad *anitos* they attributed all hardships, poverty, bad moments, illnesses, and deaths, while all good happenings were attributed to the good *anitos*.

Some deities controlled the weather and other phenomena essential to people's survival. The soul-spirits demanded respect and attention and, together with the *anitos*, could cause illness and disease. The soul-spirits, however, were not worshipped. People interacted with them as they did with the living and utmost care was undertaken not to offend them. If respect was not shown to these spirits, as in food and drink not shared with them during rituals, they would cause illness. A principle of exchange and reciprocity existed.

The arrival of the Spaniards in 1565 with their sword and cross did not automatically convert the Filipinos to Christianity, although the archipelago was apportioned among the religious orders. The first religious missionaries in the Philippines were the Augustinians, who arrived with Legazpi in 1565. The Franciscans arrived in 1577, followed by the Jesuits in 1581. The Dominicans came in 1587 and finally the Recollects in 1606. It should be noted that the introduction of the new religion coincided with the imposition of colonial sovereignty, power, and foreign control. There was strong resistance and the natives did not understand the sophisticated concepts of religion. Striking similarities between the pre-Spanish religion and Roman Catholicism, also a belief in a Supreme Being, however, may have made missionaries' work easier and the natives finally capitulated and accepted the new faith.

In general, the responses of the Filipinos to Christianity were selective. The natives reinterpreted and even rejected some Spanish religious beliefs. Circumstances gave them considerable freedom in selecting their responses to the evangelization process. Some, although accepting the new faith, continued to keep and observe their old pre-Christian beliefs. Some were practical and sensible in their acceptance of the Roman Catholic religion at face value to avoid inconveniences brought about by the periodic raids of armed troops upon their scattered villages and settlements. Author John Phelan believed that the success achieved by the religious missionaries could be ascribed, in large part, to the 'realistic adjustment they made to the limitations that geo-ethnic factors imposed on their activity.' This is probably the reason why, three centuries later, Marcelo H. del Pilar described the religion imposed on the Filipinos 'as affecting the emotion more than the intellects'.

The degree to which Filipinos understood the meaning of the Catholic doctrine was often in proportion to the density of population and the number of assigned priests. Filipinos living near the church where a resident priest was stationed showed firmer grasp of the doctrine than those living in the vicinity of the outlying *visita* or *barrio*, serviced only by an itinerant priest. As a whole, they had little grasp of the distinction between magic and the Roman Catholic belief in miracles, idolatry, and the veneration of saints and images, superstitions, and certain Catholic rituals. Many Filipinos were enticed to the new religion through the colorful rituals of the Church and they soon enthusiastically flocked to them for religious ceremonies associated with Holy Week, the feast of Corpus Christi or the patronal *fiesta* of the locality. The pomp and pageantry that characterized the elaborate ceremonies of the church's rituals contributed much to the eventual suppression of some pre-Hispanic rituals such as drinking alcohol, which missionaries identified with pagan religious observances of betrothals, weddings, and funerals.

Christianity became a most powerful vehicle of social and economic change that affected the everyday lives of the Filipinos. The Church provided Filipinos with the chance to express their indigenous artistic and engineering tradition through the construction of the massive stone churches built during the Spanish regime. The religious orders built roads to open up new mission territories and to facilitate travel from parish to parish. Many new varieties of vegetable and other plants of economic benefit were introduced to the Philippines by the Church, and the development of commercial agriculture and urban settlements were associated with the early religious historical development.One belief that persists even today is that the Church was there as a protector of the people. This idea found its root in the Spanish period. Filipino religiosity during the Spanish era was demonstrated in strong respect and veneration for the friar whom the people considered their protector against the abuses of other Spaniards. That influence over the community continues to the present.

Filipino Christianity

In Filipino Christianity, according to Fr Frank Lynch, S. J., the Roman Catholic religion reinforced community and family solidarity in many ways. Conversely, Church institutions were influenced and modified by local social patterns. A pattern of accommodation existed between the native culture and the Hispanic Christianity, and in the centuries of contact with one another, neither emerged intact and unchanged. Each influenced and altered the other, so that Christianity in the Philippines today has a spirit and flavor of its own, as distinct from Christianity in Spain, South America and the US.

The idea of community sharing is supported and expressed by attendance at official church services such as Mass on Sundays and holy days, Novenas (prayers), and the rites celebrated on the occasion of baptism, marriages and funerals. Fr Lynch observes that these activities are 'supplemented and overshadowed in socializing intensity by various folk religious ceremonies embellished and elaborated with Spanish and local folk origin.' Church activities that stimulate community solidarity include the celebrations during the Christmas season, Lenten season, commemoration of the dead, and ceremonies related to baptisms, marriages, and funerals. Christmas celebrations, a Novena or dawn Masses draw more of the community to the church at one time than any another event in the local calendar. Christmas Midnight Mass is the climax of a two-week celebration and the church is filled to overflowing. Customary gatherings at the church plaza after the Mass and the family repast after the Midnight Mass are extensions of the church activities. The first part stimulates community solidarity, while the second strengthens the family. In both cases, the religious gathering is seen in a social context.

The uniqueness of Filipino Christianity is seen in Church activities in observance of Holy Week. During the Lenten season the community is brought together through several folk religious practices with the reading of the *pasion* or staging of a passion play being the focal point. The reading or chanting of the *pasion*, according to Fr Lynch, is unique to Filipino Christian belief and akin to the pre-Spanish custom of chanting lengthy local epics. Other important activities that have strong connections with Filipino Christianity refer to what Fr Lynch called 'life-crisis ceremonies' consisting of baptisms, marriages and funerals. For instance, when a relative dies, a wake or a nine-day *padasal* (prayers for the departed) follows the burial. Customary activities held during the wake serve as a convenient framework within which the community, or part of it, can give public recognition to an individual's talent as a singer, guitarist, or perhaps an impersonator. It is also an occasion for the young men and women to come to know one another better, or publicly to taunt some blushing couple about their budding romance. On these occasions community members renew their social acquaintance with one another. Religious belief also strengthens family solidarity. In the Philippines when one speaks of the family, it should be seen in the context of the extended family, not as the nuclear family in Australia, a family with two children. The word *mag-anak* in the Filipino language refers to the immediate and a potentially extended family. There are four major occasions during the annual religious cycle that strengthen family solidarity: the town *fiesta*, Christmas Day, *undras* (All Souls Day, November 1 and 2) and Holy Week, listed here in order of importance. In all cases, far-flung members of the family make every effort to be reunited with their kin.

The town *fiesta* is a yearly celebration held on the Feast Day of the town's patron saint, and more often than not is also the name of the town and the church. As an example, out of the more than 3,000 towns and *barrios* (villages) in the country, 160 towns and *barrios* are named after San Jose (St. Joseph) and they would celebrate their *fiesta* on the same date as dictated by tradition. *Fiesta* today is composed of *fiesta* proper, which is organised and supervised by the parish priests, and the *feria,* organised by civil officials and prominent laymen. The *fiesta* proper includes church functions and church-sponsored or religious entertainment, while the *feria* includes sports, dances, plays, variety shows, raffles, beauty contests, gambling, commercial activities, and a carnival. The same structure is found in *fiesta* celebrations in the Filipino communities of Sydney, Brisbane and Melbourne. Despite the recreational aspect, the underlying nature of *fiesta* is religious.

Early Filipino society was oriented around kinship and this characteristic found its place in the Roman Catholic custom of ritual co-parenthood. The co-parenthood system, also known as *compadrazgo,* is the ritual extension of kinship. It was originally introduced into the Philippines as part of Roman Catholic ritual, to ensure that the child would be educated in the faith. According to the Roman Catholic ritual each person at baptism is required to have two sponsors, a godfather and a godmother.

Godparents or sponsors are also required for Confirmation, on the assumption that Confirmation would be the completion of baptism. Baptism has been traditionally regarded as a spiritual rebirth, as opposed to natural birth. At wedding ceremonies, godparents are optional; in the betrothal ceremony only parents are essential. Thus, a spiritual and mystical relationship is formed between the godparents and the godchild. No marriage between them, for example, is possible. As a result of this linkage, the co-parenthood system became part of Filipino culture and has taken a broader significance than simply perpetuating church doctrine. Explaining the *compadre or compadrazgo system*, Dr. Robert S. Fox said:

> The basic organizational principle ... *compadrazgo* ... functions to systematize a normative relationship between unrelated individuals (families) based upon ... kinship. The socially and emotionally secure relationships of kinship are reduplicated and extended by *compadrazgo*, a function of considerable importance in view of the potential conflict underlying all interpersonal relationships between non-kinsmen, a result of the Filipino's concept of 'self-esteem' or *hiya* ... *Compadrazgo* provides a means of ordering hierarchical relations (landlord-tenant, employer-employee, high-low status), a channel for upward mobility and possibly a mechanism of out-migration from the rural to urban areas.

This large kin group, or *compadrazgo*, is formed through the rituals of baptism, confirmation, and marriage. The non-kindred sponsors for these occasions become linked to the family and are expected to help the family, but they may also expect to be helped by the family when the occasion arises. This helping relationship is known as 'reciprocal rights and obligations', or *utang na loob*. The effect of the ritual relationship is to treat the ritual relative as if he or she were family. The co-parenthood system is an integral part of baptismal rites while wedding ceremonies bring together two extended families, symbolized and sealed by the union in the matrimony of a representative couple.

The Muslim Filipinos

Religion is often observed as a divisive force, even in the present state of society. We are reminded of many instances where conflicts and sufferings were caused by peoples' religious beliefs. This situation is also found in the Philippines between the Filipino Muslims and the Filipino Christians. The former, considered minorities in the Philippines are caught in the dilemma of having to reconcile the demands of their concept of faithfulness to Islam with their responsibilities as citizens in a modern state in which Filipino Christians predominate.

Muslim Filipinos were once the majority inhabitants of the Mindanao region. As a result of the colonization of Mindanao, however, the socio-demographic status of the Muslims has changed from a majority to a minority. The 13 cultural-linguistic groups of Muslim Filipinos are concentrated in western and southern Mindanao Island, the Sulu Archipelago, and coastal areas of southern Palawan.

Only five (Sulu, Tawi-Tawi, Lanao del Sur, Maguindanao, and Basilan) of the 22 provinces is there a Muslim majority. The Islamisation of Mindanao and Sulu resulted in an ideological bond among different groups of people in the region which led to the emergence of a new sense of ethnic identity that distinguished Muslim from non-Muslim populations of the Philippines. Islam also became a unifying force and, in the face of colonial domination, provided the basis for revolutionary action. It was this underlying ideology for resistance that conceived a *jihad* against Spanish colonialists when they arrived in the Philippines with their sword and cross in 1565. Islam had very little impact

27

upon the indigenous inhabitants of the central and northern parts of the Philippines, as they were mostly *animists*. The Spaniards converted the local inhabitants to Christianity without much resistance. The advance of Islam to the north was halted by the arrival of the Spaniards and they pushed the Muslims back to the Visayas and later to the Mindanao area, where they are concentrated today.

In Filipino society today, Muslims have managed to retain many of their traditional socio-political structures. Islam is the essence of the foundation of the Muslim society. All laws, with the exception of those which concern traditional customs, were essentially within the bounds of the *sharia*. Muslim Filipinos, from the sultan to village headman, are of religious inclination and because of this, Muslim society, as distinct from the Filipino Christian community, is governed by Islamic and customary laws and religiously inclined leaders. With this strong religious belief the Muslims have been less ready to absorb and adopt more modern ways of life, even after their inclusion into the Philippine Republic in 1946. Many Muslims regard the structure of the Filipino Government, its codes of laws and political ideas as inconsistent with the *sharia*. They possess a strong sense of group consciousness and continue to assert their identity as Muslims. The general resurgence of Islam since the end of World War II has raised Islamic consciousness among Filipino Muslims and this has increased the gap between the two groups of Filipinos who co-exist in a geographically fragmented state. The Muslims constitute a nationality distinct from and older than Christian Filipinos.

Religion and the State

The church's influence on Philippine society is pervasive. This was particularly evidenced during the administration of President

Corazon C. Aquino. The then Archbishop of Manila, the Most Reverend Jaime Cardinal Sin, compared the relationship between the Roman Catholic Church and the Philippine Government to two rails that make up a railway track. 'The Church and State relationship,' he said, 'can't be too close, neither can it be too distant.' The church's influence is reflected best in the provisions about the family in the present Constitution of the Philippines. Framed by a 50-member Constitutional Commission, a majority of whom were Roman Catholics, this declared the primacy of the family, outlawed divorce and abortion and successfully intruded into a purely government responsibility for education. The accommodation given to religious groups is also evident when one seat in the Commission was reserved for the *Iglesia ni Cristo* (Church of Christ), a local religious sect that emerged in the 1970s as a very strong political force in the Philippines, particularly during the Marcos Administration.

With the present Constitution, religious instruction is now allowed in public schools. The Church's strong grip on education, a very important tool of the church, can be considered an approximation of its hold over the minds of the Filipinos during the Spanish colonial period. At present there are operating 168 Roman Catholic colleges and universities and almost 400 Roman Catholic secondary schools, not to mention primary schools, with a total enrolment of more than half-a-million students. Added to education there is a strong Church presence in the administration of hospitals, orphanages and charitable organizations. It controls the Bank of the Philippine Islands, reputed to be one of the largest banks in the Philippines. Given this situation, the population has remained staunchly Roman Catholic and it continues to believe and to expect that the church would defend the people's rights and protect them.

On Miracles

The common conviction that miracles are part of Filipino religious belief can also be traced from pre-Spanish times. The Filipinos' belief in miracles, observes author John Phelan, was boundless and virtually uncontrollable. Another writer said that the Filipinos have a 'remarkable sense of make-believe'. Few of these 'miracles' received any official recognition from the church, but such ecclesiastical discouragement has done little to dampen the simple faith of the Filipinos in the ever-present powers of the supernatural. To this day, in the rural Philippines, an atmosphere of the miraculous and the supernatural permeates Filipinos' Roman Catholicism.

In 1993 the *Sydney Morning Herald* published an article headlined 'Filipinos Seek Miracles'. The journalist described the Philippines as a 'nation beset by poverty [which] turns more and more to the supernatural' to bring new hope and possibly a solution to its many problems. The main story in the article revolved around a 16-year old former church choir boy who claimed to have seen regularly the Virgin Mary, surrounded by singing angels. This revelation drove at least a million Filipino devotees to the barren place outside the boy's village 190 kilometers north of Manila, all waiting for a miracle, despite the skepticism shown earlier by Cardinal Sin, who said 'Sometimes people there are hungry, and when you are hungry you see visions.'

The miracle was proven to be a hoax, a product of the rich imagination and ideas of some people behind the whole scheme with the boy as the central figure. The Church Committee tasked to evaluate the Virgin apparition declared at the end that the religious miracle in the town of Agoo, La Union, north of Manila, that became a multi-million peso exercise, was 'far from being supernatural'. Also quoted in the same article was Teodoro Benigno, former press secretary of President Aquino, who said 'miracle syndrome' is deeply entrenched in Filipino culture. The so-called apparition, according to him, 'showed us the face of a nation wreathed in spiritual piety, of a people refusing to give up what they have left of their hope, of a clawing at the dark by seeking to touch the hem of Mary's apparition lighted by the dancing sun.'

The same theme was tackled in the 1980s award-winning international Filipino film *Himala,* directed by the late Ishmael Bernal and starred by Filipino dramatic actress Nora Aunor. The film, which garnered awards in international film festivals, was based on a 1967 story of a girl on the island of Cabra who was believed to be the Chosen One. It focused on the Filipino's world of desperation, poverty, sickness, death, celebrity, and religious fanaticism. The film questioned the institutions and truths Filipinos created among themselves and challenged them to do something about them. It was a serious commentary on how myth serves its purpose when truth is too hard to swallow.

The story revolves around a young girl named Elsa, a simpleton; a lowly, plain-looking lass in a remote Philippine village named Cupang. She turns the impoverished village upside down and greed triumphs for a while when she claims to have seen the apparition of the Virgin Mary and starts performing miraculous healing of the sick and desperate. Pilgrims, the sick, invalid and terminal cases, all seeking the last way to wellness, flock to what used to be an obscure and sleepy town. Some buy the religious statues of the saints in makeshift stores that mushroom near the site of the apparition or bottles of the village's holy water that an enterprising religious woman manage. Tourist money flows in freely as people troop to the site, now called "Elsa's Shrine'. And soon a brothel is doing a roaring business nearby. It is

managed by Elsa's former classmate who became a prostitute in Manila and who brought back her experience to her hometown. As the story unfolds the viewing public is confronted by faith and faithlessness, truth and delusion, as the town transforms into a bustling community. One reviewer described the film as a believable story that tackles the endless and timeless struggle of man in his quest to find something to believe in, in a country like the Philippines which is spoon-fed with Catholicism.

In the end, the young guilt ridden girl blames herself for the misfortune that has befallen her little town, the people around her, and the tragic end of the members of her family and love ones, she herself being a victim of rape. She gathers her flock and believers. She tells them she has another revelation to make. At a designated time at the site on the hill where the Virgin Mary was claimed to have appeared before her, she declares to the anticipating crowd: 'There are no miracles. They are all in our hearts. We make miracles ourselves. We pronounce a curse and we create our gods.' This is religious reality in the Philippines.

2

Filipino Symbols of Identity

In any multicultural community such as Australia, political and cultural symbols conveniently identify ethnicity. Emblems and flags, colorful and inviting food, costumes and music, customs and tradition are but a few of the dominant symbols of identity of a migrant's country of origin. This observation is also true among Filipinos, despite the wide acceptance of its Westernized cultural and political institutions.

Political symbols

The Filipino coat of arms, the national flag and anthem are the political symbols of the Philippines. They are emblematic of the form of government and illustrative of the political ideology of the people. Filipino heraldic symbols have their beginning in the first coat of arms authorized for the City of Manila through a Royal Decree issued on 20 March 1596 by King Philip II of Spain. The decree described its design as:

> ... a shield which shall have in the centre of its upper part a golden castle on a red field, closed by a blue door and windows, and which shall be surmounted by a crown; and in the lower half on a blue field a half lion and half dolphin of silver, armed and languid gules — that is to say, with red nails and tongue. The said lion shall hold in his paw a sword with guard and hilt.

After some changes in detail and other features, the seal was later adopted by the Spanish colonial government of the Philippines. Modifications and alterations were made, but the principal devices remained unaltered. During the early days of the 19th century, a new design, patterned after the National Standard of Spain, was made. The device had in the centre a *fleur-de-lis* surrounded by the quartered flag of Castille and Aragon represented by two yellow castles located on a red field and two red lions on a white field.

When the Philippine Revolution against Spain took place in 1896, two different coats of arms were simultaneously adopted by the Filipinos. Initially, Filipino leaders had no permanent political symbol. All adopted the equilateral triangle design for their coat of arms, but there was disagreement on the symbols found inside the triangle. Many documents of the *Katipunan* (the secret society that initiated the revolution against Spain) bore the letter *K* inside every angle, while the rest had the rising mythological sun in the centre. As the Tagalog word *kalayaan*, meaning 'liberty', begins with the letter K, General Artemio Ricarte, one of the high ranking Filipino revolutionary leaders, presumed that *K* stood for freedom. In 1898, the revolutionary government under General Emilio Aguinaldo finally adopted the sun and three stars as permanent symbols for their coat of arms. The official device was an equilateral triangle in the centre of which was the mythological sun with one set of eight rays and five pointed stars in each angle. The republican coat of arms had patriotic significance. The white triangle, which was of *Katipunan* origin, stood for the secret society that started the 1896 Philippine Revolution. The sun with eight rays represents the eight major provinces which took part in the fight for freedom, while the three five pointed stars symbolized Luzon, Visayas, and Mindanao, the three major geographical island groups of the Philippines.

The advent of the American military occupation in 1898 necessitated the enactment of a law prescribing a new coat of arms for the Philippines. At this time, the Manila coat of arms adopted by the Spanish colonial government was still in use and was replaced only in 1905 when the Philippine Commission approved the adoption of the new 'arms and great seal of the Philippine Islands'. The new coat of arms was designed in 1903 by Gaillard Hunt of the US State Department. It remained unaltered until the inauguration of the Commonwealth of the Philippines in 1935. It has 13 alternating white and red stripes representing the original 13 colonies of America; a chief blue above, the honor color, and over them, in an oval, the arms of Manila with the castle of Spain and the sea lion prominently displayed.

On the crest was the American eagle, the symbol of the American republic, and beneath the shield was the scroll with the words *Philippine Islands*. This design was in use until the approval of the Tydings–McDuffie Law in 1934, which promised Philippine independence after a 10-year transition period. The law, approved by the US President, ushered in a new era in the Philippines. Substantial changes in the form of government were effected. One of the last enactments of the 10th Philippine Legislature prescribed yet another symbol for the Filipinos, the arms of the great seal of the Commonwealth Government of the Philippines. Approved in 1935, the number of stripes was reduced from thirteen to two and the three five-pointed stars were added. The words *Commonwealth of the Philippines* replaced the *Philippine Islands*. The eagle of the new design was slightly enlarged and placed a little lower and closer to the arms. To achieve a more artistic piece of work, it also incorporated the modified seal of the City of Manila.

On 15 December 1938, a Special Committee of the Coat of Arms of the Philippines, under the Chairmanship of Dr. Teodoro

M. Kalaw, a Filipino scholar and historian, was created by President Manuel L. Quezon. After almost two years of study, the committee recommended certain modifications to the coat of arms of the Commonwealth of the Philippines. In particular, the committee endorsed the inclusion of the eight-rayed Philippine sun as the point of honor on the escutcheon proper, then erroneously occupied by the castle and sea lion of the old coat of arms of the City of Manila. The coat of arms of the Commonwealth of the Philippines was revised accordingly in 1940. The new design featured two stripes, blue at the right side and red on the left side of the shield; a chief white field above, studded with three five-pointed golden stars equidistant from each other and over them, on an oval, the eight-rayed sun in rayonant with each ray flanked on both sides by minor rays. On the crest is the American eagle, her right talon grasping an olive branch of eight leaves and eight fruits, and the left talon grasping three spears. Beneath the shield is the scroll with the inscription *Philippines.*

Following the spirit of providing appropriate symbols to various branches of the government, the Philippine Heraldry Committee was created by President Quezon in 1940. The Committee was assigned the task of studying and recommending the designs and symbolism of official seals of the Philippines' different political subdivisions, cities and semi-government institutions. The heraldic work of the committee was suspended during the Pacific War.

When the Japanese-sponsored government, under President Jose P. Laurel, took over the government, a more nationalistic policy was adopted. Aside from enforcing a national language, a new seal was designed. Foreign components of the Filipino heraldic symbol which previously represented its colonial links with Spain and the US were removed. The American eagle representing US authority in the Philippines and the dragon and castle symbols of the Spanish colonial past, were taken out. Instead, the salient features of the Philippine flag and the seal of the short-lived Philippine republic – the sun and the three stars located inside an equilateral triangle – were incorporated in the new design. At the centre of the triangle is the eight-rayed mythological sun. Written within the three sets of two marginal lines of the three sides of the triangle were *kalayaan* (Liberty), *kapayapaan* (Peace) and *katarungan* (Justice). Around the seal was a double marginal circle within which was written the Tagalog words *Republika ng Pilipinas (Republic of the Philippines)*.

On 7 January 1946, President Sergio Osmeña re-activated the Philippine Heraldry Committee. The body's most important accomplishment was to redesign the Filipino coat of arms. The new design was approved by the Congress of the Philippines on the eve of the inauguration of the Third Philippine Republic on 3 July 1946. It was designed by then Captain Galo B. Ocampo, a member and secretary of the committee who later became its chairman. In Ocampo's design, the Philippine Sun, no longer the mythological sun of General Aguinaldo with its eight rays, occupies the point of honor in the centre, while the three five-pointed stars, representing Luzon, Visayas and Mindanao, occupy the upper portion of the shield. On the right side, on a blue field, is the bald-headed American eagle and on the left side, on a red field, the lion rampant of Spain. Beneath the arms is a scroll with the words *Republic of the Philippines* inscribed. Appropriately enough, the new seal restored the symbols representing two dominant components of the Philippines' past — the Americans and the Spaniards.

In 1978, then President Ferdinand E. Marcos incorporated a theme into the national symbol. Marcos believed that under his government's New Society Program, the ultimate national unity of the Filipinos could be achieved through the 'active participation of every citizen' motivated by one guiding spirit. Thus, *Isang Bansa, Isang Diwa* (One Nation, One Spirit) became the national motto of the Philippines. It was immediately incorporated into the national seal, replacing the words *Republic of the Philippines* which were originally inscribed in the scroll beneath the arms. The revised design was finalized by the National Historical Institute's designer, Teodoro Atienza, and approved by the Office of the President on 31 July 1978. When the Aquino administration took over the government, with its avowed task of obliterating any Marcos contribution, bad or good, to Philippine history, the Filipino coat of arms was again altered and the national motto left out. The original design has been followed until now.

The Philippine national anthem and flag

On 12 June 1898 the Aguinaldo Mansion in Kawit, Cavite, became hallowed ground. It was on a steamy summer afternoon of that 12 June, that a jubilant crowd of revolutionists and onlookers flocked to General Emilio Aguinaldo's residence, now officially called 'the Aguinaldo Shrine', to witness a historic event — the proclamation of Filipinos' emancipation from Spanish bondage. At about 4pm, at the window facing the main highway, the Declaration of Independence was read by Judge Advocate General Ambrosio Rianzares Bautista, a trusted Aguinaldo adviser and author of the text of the proclamation. The declaration was followed by the unfurling of the Filipino national flag and the playing of the national anthem. The independence declaration, the flag, and the anthem, marked the birth of a nation, the first democratic government in South-East Asia. Earlier, the historic banner symbolizing Filipino unity was first used during the Battle of Alapan, near Kawit, on 28 May 1898. That historic event is now celebrated in the Philippines as National Flag Day. Recalling the triumph in his memoirs, General Aguinaldo said:

The combat lasted from ten in the morning until three in the afternoon, and through lack of ammunition the Spaniards surrendered with all their arms to the Filipino revolutionists, who entered Cavite with the prisoners. I seized upon this glorious occasion to bring out and unfurl the national flag, which was saluted by an immense multitude with acclamations of delirious joy and great hurrahs for Philippine independence and for the generosity of the United States, the act being witnessed by various officials and marines of the American squadron, who demonstrated clearly their sympathy with the cause of the Filipinos by taking part in their natural jubilee.

The National Flag

The Filipino flag was design by General Aguinaldo himself and sewn in Hong Kong by Marcela Mariño Agoncillo, wife of Felipe Agoncillo, a leading diplomat in the Aguinaldo Government. The Agoncillo family left for Hong Kong in 1896 to escape Spanish persecution. In making the flag, Marcela was assisted by her seven-year old daughter Lorenza, and Delfina Herbosa de Natividad, niece of Jose Rizal. It took them five days to complete the important task. Years later, Marcela Agoncillo described her feeling about sewing the historic flag as 'of utmost love and joy'.

The flag had a rectangular design with its left portion dominated by a white equilateral triangle. A horizontal blue stripe above and red below of the remaining portion of the flag were clearly shown. Inside the white triangle, in the centre, was the eight-rayed mythological golden sun and on each corner of the triangle was a five-pointed star. The eight rays of the golden sun represent the first eight provinces that initiated the 1896 Philippine revolution, while the three five-pointed stars stand for the three major geographical subdivisions that comprise the Philippines: Luzon, Visayas and Mindanao. The red stripe of the flag stands for the willingness of the Filipinos to shed blood in defense of their country, while the blue stripe symbolizes universality and noble aspiration of the Filipinos. The Philippine flag is said to be the only flag in the world which could show whether the nation is at peace or at war by inverting the position of the flag.

The present national flag of the Filipinos was not a result of an accident of history. It reflects the traditions and ideals of the people. As an emblem, it passed various stages of evolution during the two phases of the Philippine campaign for freedom, namely from Balintawak to Biyak-na-Bato (1896 to 1897) and from Kawit to the Commonwealth government (1898 to 1936). The first flag in the evolution of the national banner was the Katipunan War Standard consisting of a red rectangular design with three white *K*s, the *Katipunan* symbol, written and arranged in the form of a triangle at its centre. This was followed by General Mariano Llanera's so-called 'Skull Flag' which was used by his men in Nueva Ecija at the beginning of the 1896 Revolution. The Llanera Flag was a black rectangular cloth inscribed with a big letter *K* on the right and the human skull and crossbones on the left, all in white. The third stagew as represented by another Katipunan War Flag, with the three *K*s, in white, arranged horizontally at the middle of a red rectangular design.

The General Pio del Pilar flag, also a red rectangular flag, had a white triangle at the left and on each corner of the equilateral triangle was inscribed the three *K*s. At the centre of this triangle was a design of a half-sun rising with eight rays. All the symbols found inside the white triangle were in red. The del Pilar Flag was followed by the Bonifacio War Standard, a red rectangular flag with three white *K*s arranged horizontally and a sun with an irregular number of rays, also in white. Next was the reformed

Katipunan War Standard, a red rectangular piece of cloth with a variant design of the sun, also with eight rays; inside was the letter *K* written in the old Tagalog script, for *kalayaan* or freedom. This flag was again revised during the 1897 Naic Convention with the mythological 'Sun of Liberty' as its main feature. The next flag, known as the General Gregorio del Pilar Flag, is unique in the sense that it was the forerunner of the present Filipino Flag. This banner had a red horizontal stripe above and black stripe below, with a blue equal-sided triangle on its left. The Aguinaldo flag, made by Marcela Agoncillo in Hong Kong and unfurled officially during the proclamation of the independence of the Filipinos on 12 June 1898, had some features of the present flag. The one difference was the mythological sun which is not depicted in the present flag. The current description and specifications of the Filipino flag followed a presidential directive issued in 1936 by then President Quezon. The same description and specifications have been adopted by subsequent Philippine Constitutions between 1946 and 1987.

The National Anthem

The National anthem of the Philippines was originally a march envisioned by General Aguinaldo as a musical piece that 'can inspire our men to fight the enemy – something which embodies the noble ideals of our race.' Julian Felipe, a music teacher and composer from Cavite City, was assigned the task. On 11 June, the day before the declaration of Filipino independence, Felipe played his masterpiece. General Aguinaldo and his military leaders applauded the beautiful march and called it *Marcha Nacional Filipina* (Philippine National March). In the presence of such military officers as General Mariano Trias and Secretary of War, Baldomero Aguinaldo, Felipe's composition was ap-

approved as the national hymn of the country. For the first time the public heard the soul-inspiring piece. Without a lyric, however, the national anthem was of little use to patriots at home or in the battle field.

In August 1899, Jose Palma, a poet-soldier and younger brother of Rizal's contemporary, Filipino nationalist Rafael Palma, wrote *Filipinas*, a patriotic poem in elegant and sonorous Spanish. The poem, published in *La Independencia* in September 1899, fitted the music of the *Marcha Naciónal Filipina* and became the lyric of the national anthem. The original Spanish text of the Philippine national anthem was jointly translated into English by A. L. Lane, an American, and Camilo Osias, a Filipino educator and later a senator. Today, it is mainly sung in its Filipino translation approved by the Institute of National Language (now the Commission on Filipino Language), and called *Pambansang Awit*, not *Lupang Hinirang* as many insist on calling it.

Pambansang Awit*

Bayang magiliw
Perlas ng Silanganan
Alab ng Puso
Sa dibdib mo'y buhay.

Lupang hinirang
Duyan ka ng magiting
Sa manlulupig
Di ka pasisiil.

Sa dagat at bundok
Sa simoy at sa langit mong bughaw
May dilag ang tula

At langit sa paglayang minamahal.
Ang kislap ng watawat mo'y
Tagumpay na nagniningning
Ang bituin at araw mo
Kaylan pa ma'y di magdidilim.

Lupa ng araw
Ng l'walhati't pagsinta
Buhay ay langit sa piling mo.
Aming ligaya
Na pag may mang-aapi
Ang mamatay nang dahil sa iyo.

*Official version in Filipino and being used since 1956

42

Filipino national costumes

The ethnicity of migrants is almost always identified through their own languages, songs, food, personal surnames, and traditional or native costumes. This is also true among Filipinos in Australia. Like other frontiers of foreign influences, however, Filipino cultural symbols are not free from outside attribution. As a matter of fact, in their colonial experience, Filipinos were able to synthesize foreign influences into distinct Filipino symbols.

The Philippines' national costumes are called *terno*, for the ladies, and *barong*, for men. They are products of varied cultural foreign designs, examples of integrating local and external elements. Over the years both costumes have developed into unique symbols that identify the country of origin of Filipinos overseas, including those in Australia. In Caruana's *Filipinos in Western Sydney*, a community profile published by the New South Wales Department of School Education in September, 1993, Filipino identity –was highlighted by featuring on its cover Filipinos in their 'native' costumes.

The Terno

Like many features of Filipino cultural identity, the national costumes have undergone major changes brought about by foreign fashion ideas. But the *terno* maintains its unique butterfly sleeves which emphasize the femininity of its wearer. In 1879, J. de Man, a Belgian visitor to Manila, described the ordinary Filipino women's attire as 'a kind of skirt, widely checked or striped in bold colors of red, blue or yellow, and [with] a short jacket that more or less resembles what European women call a *mariniere* or sailor.' The cloth was made of 'white cotton, very light, washed and ironed with great care, and transparent'. In one of the countless parties he attended, de Man observed the *mestizas* (Spanish–Filipina or Chinese–Filipina women). He considered them as 'very attractive and yield nothing in pulchritude to the most beautiful women of Europe'. He attributed this, partly, to their native costumes. The Filipino attire for women, even during colonial times, was already considered a unique, delicate costume. Its uniqueness sprung from its loose, soft flowing sleeves, and starched and folded collar-scarf called *pañuelo*. The skirts were of various colors, usually made of imported materials.

Two main annual religious events – Christmas and Lent – provided the opportunity for Filipina women to wear their unique native attire. Having plenty of time to prepare for these annual events, and as a lot of Filipina women had mastered the art of embroidery, the cut of their sleeves became wider and wider to accommodate more embroidery pattern and designs.

The dress of Filipina women during the Spanish period consisted of a skirt with a short train supported by 'crinolines and petticoats'. It had broad stripes or checks in bright colors. A small apron of black silk was tied around the waist and the jacket or *mariniere* was short and made of light, transparent material. The jacket and short, wide, floating sleeves was a contrast to the skirt because of its rich embroidery in gold or silver thread. A tiny scarf or cravat, the principal item encrusted with brilliant stones against a dark background, completed the costumes. This accessory added 'animation to the already expressive features of the wearer and heightens the beauty of her normally shining long hair'.

In 1889, the most popular Spanish-influenced Filipino attire was introduced. Presently known as 'Maria Clara', the skirt, usually of heavy satin, was cut in numerous panels in contrasting colours. The *camisa* or upper part of the attire had delicately embroidered, wide-bell-shaped sleeves gathered on the upper armhole. The *pañuelo* was placed on the neckline, falling softly to drape the shoulders. At about the turn of the 19th century, some radical changes in the costume took place. The *camisa* became shorter and the *pañuelo* achieved wider proportion, making it more of an accessory than a cover up for modesty. However, to an American observer in 1901, the Filipino costume was not 'especially attractive' but unusual. 'It consists of a flowing cotton skirt, transparent blouse with immense sleeves, showing the chemisette beneath, and a starched neck-piece called the *pañuelo*', he wrote.

The advent of the Americans brought many changes to the Philippines, particularly to Filipina women who actively participated in various undertakings. Their new roles in the community called for a shorter *camisa* to facilitate movement. These changes in the Filipino attire for women eventually gave birth to the *terno*. Appropriately enough, local materials such as *jusi* (pinapple mixed with abaca fibre), *piña* (pineapple fibre), and *sinamay* (abaca cloth – manila hemp) were considered suitable materials. During the second decade of American occupation, the *terno* became slimmer and mostly made of imported materials. The famous annual national Philippine Carnival became a showcase of the *terno* because it had to be shown in such extravagance and fancy. As Filipina women, during the succeeding years, achieved significant roles in political affairs and other fields of endeavor, adjustment of the costume to their needs took place. The upper part of the dress and skirt were joined together and the butterfly sleeves were conveniently attached to the armholes.

The most controversial event relating to the *terno* happened during the first Philippine Carnival in 1908 where the reigning queen, Pura Villanueva, who later became the wife of scholar and historian, Teodoro M. Kalaw, and mother to former Senator

Maria Kalaw-Katigbak, wore the first *terno* without the obligatory *pañuelo*. The event stirred the fashion-conscious women of Manila's high society. But it paved the way for a more practical cut and design that revolutionized the pattern of the *terno*. It was accepted rapidly. During World War II the popularity of the *terno* declined. Despite the nationalistic policy of the Japanese-sponsored Philippine government, support for the *terno* waned, perhaps because of the difficult economic situation. In the 1960s, the flawless construction and proper setting of the butterfly sleeves became the ultimate gauge in judging a successfully made *terno*. By 1978, the national costume for women reached the height of its development and could no longer afford further changes; otherwise its uniqueness would disappear. It was at about that time that the *terno* was given a new treatment. Its butterfly sleeves achieved that 'sculptured look', evident in its clear lines and firm modern style of construction.

The popularity of the *terno* reached its peak when then First Lady Imelda Romualdez Marcos, using ethnic features of Filipino culture to her advantage, was almost always seen wearing different designs of the *terno*. Soon, her kind of butterfly sleeves, a little bit smaller than the usual *terno*, became popular and many referred to it as the *Imelda terno look*. For almost two decades the *Imelda look* became a permanent fixture in official government functions. In many of her numerous cultural commitments, Mrs. Marcos always wore a *terno*, to project her strong support for Filipino *haute couture*. The new *terno* was given wide exposure, particularly during Mrs. Marcos' meeting with world leaders such as China's ailing leader, Mao Zedong, His Majesty King Fahd of Saudi Arabia, Soviet Foreign Minister Andrei Gromyko, and others. In 1982, during the US official state visit of the Filipino first couple, Mrs. Marcos wore a yellow colored flowing *terno* at the White House ceremonies and many admired her delicate appearance. A resplendent pale red *terno* was also adored at the State Dinner given in their honor at the White House by US President Ronald Reagan and First Lady Nancy Reagan. More photos of Mrs. Marcos wearing other *ternos* in different hues were published in major dailies in the US and syndicated throughout the world. Particularly attractive was the delicate dark violet colored *terno* she was wearing when the Marcoses paid a courtesy call on US Defense Secretary, Caspar Weinberger. Many of Mrs. Marcos' *terno* were left in Malacañang Palace when the Marcoses fled the country in 1986 and are now a major attraction, second only in popularity to the 3,000 plus Imelda shoes, at the converted Malacañang Palace Museum.

Female Filipino diplomats and government representatives overseas have adopted unofficially the example of Mrs. Marcos. Four Filipino women diplomats, recognized in their respective fields of expertise, have added glamour to their official duties by wearing the *terno* at various social activities they were obliged to attend. Particularly popular in their *ternos* were former Philippine Ambassador to Australia, Leticia Ramos-Shahani, who was UN Assistant Secretary General for Social Development and Humanitarian Affairs in 1975, and Ambassador Helena S. Benitez, 1966 chairperson of the Commission on the Status of Women. The late Dr Estefania Aldaba-Lim, UN Special Representative for the International Year of the Child in 1977-1979, and 1985 UN chairperson of the Commission on the Status of Women, Ambassador Rosario Gonzales-Manalo, were also seen proudly wearing their favorite *ternos*. Today, the *terno* is used mainly during formal or semi-formal occasions, particularly in official ceremonies hosted by the government.

Like many Asians, Filipinos have their regional costumes that show their local geographical origin. For the women of Luzon, the *balintawak* or *baro at saya*; the Visayan women, the *patadyong*; and the Muslim women, light-fitting trousers with *malong* draped over one shoulder and wrapped around the body in a *sari* fashion.

The Barong

As another Filipino cultural symbol, the *barong* for men has undergone major changes, too. These were brought about by foreign influences, but the *barong,* since it first appeared in 1770, retains its elaborate design, a cool, lightweight, classic shirt appropriate for the tropics. The *barong*, originally worn by *barrio* officials during the Spanish colonial period, underwent radical changes in cut and materials, but it has always been a long-sleeved attire with cuffs and worn tucked out over a *camisa chino*. The *barong* has a distinctive design and raised embroidery of varying richness on the half-open chest with buttons. It is normally made of *piña, jusi*, or *sinamay*. As a result of a later search for a better substitute, however, *ramie* fibre (from a shrub) has now been accepted as an alternative material for this national symbol. Since the early 1980s, ordinary Filipinos prefer *jusilyn*, a combination of cotton and polyester, for making the *barong* because of its affordable cost and its crease-resistance.

In the late 1960s, the *barong*, as formal attire, was tailored very much like a Western coat with wide lapels, pockets, and with wide button-less cuffs. The only semblance to the traditional *barong* was the fabric – a transparent fine *ramie*. The early *barong* was designed as long-sleeved attire, with a lower front uncut and the upper portion, or what is called the 'pechera', open and with buttons. Elaborate design was the distinction of the 'pechera'. The cuffs, too, had the same unusual designs and were fastened with cuff links that, among the moneyed, came in gold, silver, or costly stones.

Jean Mallat, a French physician who worked for the San Juan de Dios Hospital in Intramuros, Manila, betwen 1840 and 1846, described the *barong* as either plain or embroidered and of *sinamay* or *piña* cloth and heavily starched. Mallat also recalled that the shirt reached below the knees and was always worn outside black or bluish silk pants. During the late 1880s, the *barong* came in coat-form, made of much cruder fabric and less tailored. Then there was the variant *barong* called *pinukpuk*. It was a collarless, long-sleeved shirt made of crude materials. A more radical modification of the *pinukpuk* appeared briefly with a collar in a ruffled style. Despite this modification, however, the collarless *barong* continued its popularity until the early 1890s.

The ruffled collarless *barong* preceded the coat-style design and more changes took place when the ruffled collar became plain and the *barong* was worn outside the trousers over a *camisa chino* and under a European topcoat. This style was made popular by sons of Filipino middle class families who visited and studied in Europe during the mid-19th century. Soon the 'cerrada' or the close-necked *barong* became fashionable and the buttons on the cuffs disappeared. The ruffled collar, with a more elaborate design, and the ruffled cuffs re-appeared in 1896. They were in vogue until 1920, when the most authentic design of the *barong* appeared, and it was made of *rengue* abaca fibre, as it is known today. It was worn over a *camisa chino* and had a design based on a half-open chest and a plain collar. This design and form lasted until the 1930s. One criticism against the *barong* is that it is easily wrinkled. Dante Ramirez, a well-known Manila fashion designer, said 'it's awful when we perspire and the shirt starts to show visible wrinkles or folds'. But nothing could be said against the 'comfort and ease the wearer experienced even through the hottest or busiest days', Ramirez added.

More modern fashion ideas have influenced the design of the *barong*. One of them was the Cardin-style *barong* which was designed by French fashion designer Pierre Cardin in 1970. Cardin improvised the cuffs and the 'pechera' and made the body tapered. The new *barong* look became very popular not only among Filipinos, but among international celebrities like world-renown pianist Van Cliburn and Hollywood actor George Hamilton, who wore their *barong* during their sojourns in the Philippines. When American actor Gregory Peck visited Manila a few decades ago, he wore his delicately embroidered *barong* tucked in under his black evening suit. He was a sensation among the members of the Manila high society. It was acceptable because of his stature — an international celebrity experimenting with the local *haute couture*; otherwise, the *barong* tucked in was unacceptable, even among the most Westernised Filipinos. During the late 1970s, at a diplomatic reception in Singapore, then Prime Minister Lee Kuan Yew was reported as greeting his guests wearing the *barong*. Observers were not surprised, knowing that Singapore has a similar climate year-round like Manila. When then Australian Minister for Immigration Al Grassby visited Manila in 1974, he was presented with an embroidered *barong*. It created a sensation when Minister Grassby appeared in the Australian Parliament dressed in the elegant white Philippine *barong* to vote in a division.

Because of international exposure, the *barong* gained new patrons, mostly higher government officials and business executives, who started to wear the native attire in the new design and cut. Pitoy Moreno, a leading Filipino couturier, observed early in the 1980s that the *barong* 'has become a popular export commodity to European resorts'. It has been seen in New York, Madrid and Switzerland as a dress shirt. Thus, another decline in the use of the old-styled *barong* took place.

The popularity of the *barong* as an official attire was started by Philippine President Ramon Magsaysay in the early 1950s and was enhanced during the Marcos era when President Marcos himself was always seen wearing the *barong*. He was pictured wearing the *barong* in his daily round of government commitments, including 'official receptions in honor of foreign guests and dignitaries. More than two decades of the Marcos administration brought the *barong* to the forefront of Filipino *haute couture*. It was recognized as official and practical attire in a tropical climate. Among Filipino diplomats, who followed the example of President Marcos, the *barong* became *de rigueur* at the many official functions attended by them as ambassadors and ministers overseas. As a matter of fact, many of them were in their best *barong* when they presented their credentials to receiving foreign governments. During the 1996 APEC meeting held in Subic Bay, Philippines, leaders from the 19-member APEC Forum turned up for their annual trade summit in *barong*, the traditional Philippine shirt. The see-through *barong* shirts worn by the leaders were embroidered with designs based on Philippine window architecture and geometric shapes of rice paddies to represent APEC as a window on the Asia-Pacific. Many of the world leaders were comfortable with the shirt. No less than US President Bill Clinton described the attire as 'cool and airy'.

Today, unlike other Filipino cultural symbols such as the *terno* and the regional costumes which are used mainly during formal or semi-formal occasions hosted by the government, the *barong* has become an almost everyday article of clothing of business executives and government officials and employees in the Philippines. The significance of the *barong* as a cultural symbol is therefore not lost. This could be the reason why Felice Santa Maria, an authority on Filipino culture, regarded the *barong* as 'proof of a courageous and creative ancestry.'

President Ramon Magsaysay started the use of *barong* in official and other formal occasions. NHI Photo

Lessons from
American Democracy

American troops departing for the Philippines in 1898. NHI Photo

3

American expansion to the Pacific

'Our institutions will follow our flag on the wings of
commerce. And American law, American order,
American civilization, and the American flag will plant
themselves on shores hitherto bloody and benighted,'
Senator A. J. Beveridge

In April 1898, America declared war against Spain. The conflict
which became known as the Spanish-American War lasted one
hundred and thirteen days. The Americans won the war and as
a consequence inherited Puerto Rico, Guam, and the Philippines,
as booties of war. The acquisition of the Spanish colonies
signaled the territorial expansion of the United States, outside its
boundary, into the Pacific.

Indeed, the period between 1898 and 1902 was a turning
point in the development of America as a world power. It was
the birth of an empire and the emergence of the United States as
a paramount world power. America at last was recognized and
accorded a status of a colonial power, the same stature given to
Germany, France, Great Britain, Russia and Japan, the ruling
imperial powers of the period. However, the push beyond the
continental boundaries into Asia and the Pacific and the
attainment of its imperial status produced long term
consequences, not only for American citizens but also for the
inhabitants of the lands the United States dominated.

For one, the inclusion of the Philippines in the American empire became one of the burning issues in American politics at the beginning of the 20th century. It was a question that encompassed political, economic, moral, racial and social issues. As a nation, the United States rose from relative isolation to take its place and responsibility and became an influential force in world affairs. After a short period of waiting and hesitation, the United States through its military, maritime, financial and political resources, decided 'to have a voice in re-shaping the world's political order.'

In competing for international influence and colonies in the late 19th century, the US reached for and established itself as a giant and dominant economic power, not only in Asia but in Latin America, as well.

Looking back over a little more than a hundred years, American history is characterized by continuous territorial expansion that affected the lives of many non-white victims, like the native American Indians, Spanish and French creoles, Mexican pioneers, Cubans, Puerto Ricans, Samoans, Guamanians, Hawaiians, Filipinos and other Pacific islanders. In building its empire, the United States had added contiguous, as well as non-contiguous territories to its original map. In continental America, for instance, within a span of less than a hundred years, a marvelous expansion from the Applachians to the Pacific took place. The early American settlers initially occupied the Atlantic coast and soon after secured Kentucky and the Northwest territories. Louisiana was purchased from France in 1803 and Florida was ceded from Spain in 1813. As a result of war with Mexico in 1848, the greater west and Mexican California became part of the United States. In 1867, Alaska was acquired.

Meanwhile, the internal focus of attention within the American continent until the early part of 1898, kept the United States out of the race for colonial possessions beyond its boundary. The penetration of the under populated areas of the American continent was considered by the majority as a 'natural' act, although succeeding events indicated that the expansion across the vast American continent and finally out into the Pacific was driven by capitalism.

On the other hand, territorial acquisition beyond contiguous areas was viewed in a different light. In his book *Benevolent Assimilation:The American Conquest of the Philippines, 1898-1903*, Stuart Creighton Miller commented that 'it was this link between the extension of democracy and the westward march that made it easier for Americans to view innocently their bloody conquest of the Philippines [and other non-contiguous territories] as a continuation of the western expansion of democracy.'

In 1890, the Americans, in the word of military strategist and great apostle of American expansionism, Alfred Thayer Mahan, were 'looking outward' beyond their horizon. At that stage, America had no colonial territories of its own. Its products were not guaranteed foreign markets and its overseas markets were not protected. Its maritime strength was no match compared to Great Britain, France or Germany.

On the sidelines, America was strongly nurturing the spirit of adventure and this 'mission of civilization' was a force that was waiting in the wings. When the Spanish-American War came, it was viewed as a heaven-sent opportunity to enter the race for colonies. The urge to become an imperial power took an unprecedented upsurge. Many authorities on the subject agreed that the American industrial revolution provided the impetus for the United States to enter the global stage by the end of the 19th century.

It is impossible for anyone who has studied American history not to be amazed by the rapidity of American industrial development in the 1880s. It was swift and precise. The imperial surge followed an era of very impressive post-Civil war economic growth and activity, with American corporations and monopolies playing important parts. By the end of the 1890s, American agricultural and industrial productivity, supported by advanced technological know how, had surpassed the leading industrialized countries of Europe.

Meanwhile, across the Atlantic, European powers were scrambling for colonies, protectorates and spheres of influence. The Europeans penetrated the Indo-Chinese peninsula and the struggle for spheres of influence in China followed. The Chinese empire was transformed into a multilateral protectorate, guaranteed by the leading industrialized countries of the world.

There was a strong belief among the imperial powers that civilization was their responsibility and it was their duty to acquire colonies, colonize, and subjugate people they believed to be of inferior race. Modern military technology became the instrument of the West in carrying out their self-assumed mission. This development in Europe favored the Americans who considered their own political and economic progress as a manifestation of the role they had to play in leading people who were 'racially inferior.' There was a strong faith in the superiority of the Anglo-Saxon race and the excellence and majesty of American political institutions. This common American belief is best illustrated by American Senator Albert J. Beveridge who said in 1897 that '... we are a conquering race, and that we must obey our blood and occupy new markets and new lands.'

Senator Beveridge added that 'fate has written our policy for us; and trade of the world must and shall be ours. And we will get it as our mother [England] has told us how. We will establish trading posts through the world as distributing points for American products. We will cover the ocean with our merchant marine. We will build a navy to the measure of our greatness... Our institutions will follow our flag on the wings of commerce. And American law, American order, American civilization, and the American flag will plant themselves on shores hitherto bloody and benighted.'

The events that followed pushed the United States outside of its boundary towards the Pacific. America took the 'white man's burden' as its Messianic responsibility. A new spirit of self-assertiveness dominated the American national psyche at the close of the 19th century.

In achieving its national goal, the US was guided by the belief that national greatness, racial supremacy, commercial prosperity, military security, and territorial expansion could go hand in hand. Although clothed with altruistic missions, the underlying reason to expand outside continental America was the need for foreign markets for American products. Describing the political situation during the period, author Theodore Green said that 'in this sudden demand for foreign markets, for manufacturers and for investments that imperialism became a political policy and practice of the ruling political party in America.'

Between 1899 and 1901, four major international issues reached crises proportion in the world political arena. The United States responded to them in accordance with its new found role as a world power. The global issues concerning the administration of Samoa in Oceania, the Boxer Rebellion in China, the Boer War in South Africa, and the American control of the trans-isthmian Canal in Central America. Between 1898 and 1946, Hawaii, Puerto Rico, the Virgin Islands, Samoa and the Philippines became American territorial possessions. The Trust Territory of the Pacific Islands came, finally, in 1947.

The Philippines: An American Dilemma

After the Spanish-American War in 1898, the United States, an emerging world power, acquired Puerto Rico, Guam and the Philippines as colonies. It was a chance 'to have a voice in re-shaping the world's political order.' The new status was not a surprise to many Americans. After all, they had a common belief that it was a destiny of the United States to become a great nation. Colonizing Puerto Rico and Guam did not pose a problem. However, the Philippines caused immense trouble, not only for the American leadership, but, also for the public, as well. The Philippine problem persisted for many years.

History tells us that after this 'little war' of more than a hundred days, the Filipinos were sold like herded cows to the United States by Spain at a bargain price of almost two dollars per head. The Filipino-American War that followed the announcement of American acquisition of the Philippines lasted three years. The conflict which American authorities officially called the 'Philippine insurrection' required 126,500 American soldiers to fight the Filipinos.

At the end of the war, 4,200 American soldiers had died, 3,000 were wounded, and at a cost of nearly $200M, ten times more than the amount paid by the United States to acquire the Philippines from Spain. There were 16,000 Filipinos who perished in the one-sided 2,801 armed battles of the war, while 200,000 inhabitants died due to war related causes, including the dreaded American 'reconcentration' policy, one of the very reasons why the Americans went to war with Spain in 1898 to fight for the interest of the Cubans who suffered so much at the hands of the Spanish authorities.

As generally perceived by the Americans, the United States altruistically went to war to liberate Cuba, Puerto Rico and the

Philippines from Spanish domination and iron rule. With American victory came the urgent problem of deciding what to do with the conquered Spanish territories, principally Cuba and the Philippines.

Under the armistice protocol that suspended hostilities between Spain and the United States, Spain relinquished her sovereignty over Cuba; ceded Puerto Rico and other islands in the West Indies and the Ladrones; and evacuated Cuba, Puerto Rico and other Spanish islands. As regards the Philippines, the United States was given only limited control: 'to occupy and hold the city, bay, and harbor of Manila, pending the conclusion of a treaty of peace which shall determine the control, disposition, and government of the Philippines.

The annexation of Hawaii in the middle of 1898 was completed without any problem. And shortly after, the destinies of Cuba and Puerto Rico were decided. However, the Philippines became a dilemma, a burning issue of the day, and polarized the Americans. The Philippine question was especially difficult because of the involvement of a large number of influential and well-known leaders demanding that the Philippines be placed under American control. The issue divided a country still experiencing the euphoria of a victorious defender of the downtrodden. The division was between the imperialists and the anti-imperialists camps.

President William McKinley, who belonged to the imperialists, was initially critical of territorial acquisition and considered expansionist policy as 'criminal aggression.' He, however, capitulated to the wishes of the majority. In the end, he advocated the acquisition of the Philippines.

On the other side of the coin, the anti-imperialists believed strongly that the Philippines should be given full and immediate independence because America had no legal rights to acquire the islands. Senator William Jennings Bryan, who was defeated by McKinley during the 1900 Presidential election, was a member of this group. A respected anti-imperialist historian, Henry Adams, echoed the sentiment of the anti-imperialist group when he said: 'I turn green in bed at midnight when I think of the horror of a year's war in the Philippines... we must slaughter a million or two of foolish Malays in order to give them the comforts of flannel petticoats and electric railways.'

A smaller, third group, however, suggested combining both independence and American control, like self-governing Filipinos but with the United States enjoying a favored trade and economic position.

The controversy surrounding the acquisition of the Philippines by the Americans was the subject of countless debates and arguments between the two leading factions. Most of the arguments were focused on political process, diplomacy, rationality of imperialism, colonial motivation, the problem of change and continuity, and expansionist tradition and morality.

The imperialist camp made no secret of its conviction that the Philippines were vital to the growing American economic empire. With the annexation of Wake, Midway and the Hawaii groups in the Pacific, the Philippines provided the final strand that completed a chain of stepping stones to the lucrative markets of Asia.

Senator Albert Beveridge, in a Senate speech, best summed up the contemporary reality when he stated, with full conviction, that 'the power that ruled the Pacific in the 20th century was the power that would rule the world.'

He was frank when he added that 'with the Philippines, that power is and will forever be, the American Republic.' The presence of the Americans in the Philippines, according to the lawmaker, was to protect the Filipinos from European predators waiting in the wings for an American withdrawal and to tutor the Filipinos the rudiments of American democracy.

At the centre of the Philippine dilemma was President McKinley, a well intentioned, conservative politician, closely identified with American business with interests in building a world commercial empire, particularly in Asia and Latin America.

Historian David Haward Bain described McKinley as 'genial, ambiguous, long winded former congressman from Ohio, an enigmatic figure of limited ambition.' Bain added that the American president 'holds no values dearer or more complex than protectionism and patriotism and lastly a weak politician.' Contemporary political observers strongly believed that McKinley was catapulted to the presidency in 1896 through the help of the business community, the same group who pushed him to the war with Spain.

Given this background, it was not therefore a surprise that McKinley decided to take the 'white man's burden' and annexed the Philippines, even before the Paris negotiation had started to determine what to do with the Philippines.

To ensure smoother realization of his goal and commitment to the expansionist group, President McKinley formed a five-man body, the American negotiating panel for the Paris peace talks. Three senators were appointed to help determine the terms of the Treaty of Peace with Spain. Two were known Republican expansionists: Minnesota's Senator Cushman K. Davis, who was concurrently head of the Senate Foreign Relations Committee, and Maine's Senator William P. Frye. To balance the membership of the negotiating body, an anti-expansionist, Senator George Gray, representing the opposition, was appointed.

Secretary of State William R. Day, a close associate of President McKinley, chaired the Peace Commission, while Whitelaw Reid, an influential journalist, editor of the *New York*

Tribune and a diplomat, also a close friend of President McKinley, became the last member to join the group. Reid who represented the private sector, was also an ardent expansionist. He was said to have told, in 1896, then newly elected President McKinley that '... some day we will have Cuba, as well as the Sandwich Islands (Hawaii). To that extent, I believe in Manifest Destiny.'

When President McKinley consulted the people about the Philippine problem during his Midwest tour of the United States, public endorsement of his acquisition policy was surprisingly strong. In many of his speeches and meetings with party leaders, McKinley emphasized the strong call of duty, the wish to uplift and civilize the Filipinos. Undeniably, behind all these discourses was the stronger call of the reality that American interests in international politics, commerce, military strategy and the whole future of the Pacific basin were at stake. American diplomatic isolation must come to an end. It was inevitable and the United States must now accept the responsibility of a leading imperial power.

President McKinley was careful in his public utterances; his instructions to the Peace Commission and even within his own political party and administration were carefully worded. The American president allowed himself to be 'persuaded' in taking all of the Philippines, instead of just Mindanao or Luzon as possible American military bases. During the same period, the annexation of Hawaii was another significant issue that occupied the McKinley administration. By July of 1898, while the war was still raging, he signed the congressional resolution annexing Hawaii, heavily invoking America's 'manifest destiny.'

Evidently, strong public support was already behind him. Describing McKinley's strategy during this period of 'indecision' over the Philippine issue, historian H. Wayne claimed that, drawing opinions from other men was a favorite weapon of McKinley in making important decision.

On 16 September 1898, the United States' official stand on the Philippine issue was revealed. In his instruction to the Peace Commission, President McKinley stated that the American military presence in Manila imposes obligations on the part of the United States which cannot be ignored. Also, he underscored the new duties and responsibilities brought by the war and the obligations of America whose growth was based on advancing Western civilization.

Emphasizing further the main reason for the decision to acquire the Philippines, President McKinley told the members of the Peace Commission: 'Incidental to our tenure in the Philippines is the commercial opportunity to which American statesmanship cannot be indifferent. It is just to use every legitimate means for the enlargement of American trade; but we seek no advantages in the Orient which are not common to all.'

The German Philippines that never was

Had the United States left the Philippines alone during the Spanish-American War, the country would have fallen just the same to the other colonial powers of the period.

Cuba's liberation from Spain was America's main reason in going to war. The Philippines, being a Spanish colony in Asia where the Untied States did not have a permanent foothold, was dragged into the conflict as a battlefield. Foremost of the Untied States' rivals in replacing Spanish rule in the archipelago was Otto von Bismarck's Germany. The European power was as ready as the Americans in occupying the islands, with its naval might in the Far East waiting for signal. The Germans had just joined the splurge in partitioning China, along with the British, Russians, French and Americans.

Before the outbreak of the Spanish-American War, there were already rumors in Manila of German sympathy towards the Tagalog rebels. A number of Filipino creoles were, in fact, convicted of treason and later executed by Spanish authorities for reportedly working for the Germans.

Germany's colonial expansionist policy was felt after the Franco-Prussian War of 1870-71, whereupon she encouraged France to embark on its colonialism in Africa and Asia to divert French attention from Europe. It was not long, however, before France became engrossed with its overseas acquisition, with Great Britain as the only major rival. Germany was disturbed. She could not let herself be left out of the colonial rat race. On 24 April 1884, the first sign of Germany's colonial design manifested itself. She placed under her Imperial wings the different establishments of a German merchant in South West Africa and then followed this action with a series of successful colonial campaigns in Africa and the Pacific. Within six years, unified Germany under Bismarck had set up an empire with territories mostly in Africa. Her overseas possessions were, however, fragmented. She had scattered territories, mostly the remnant areas of colonization.

From 1890 to the outbreak of the Spanish-American War in 1898, there was a lull in Germany's colonial campaigns. It appears that she was waiting for opportunities, while closely watching developments in the colonies of the dwindling powers of Spain, China and Turkey. In 1898, Prince Bernhard von Bulow assumed the post of German foreign minister and was at the same time the foremost political adviser to the German Emperor. In a brief span of time, he activated Germany's colonial intentions. On 1 November 1897, two German missionaries were murdered in China. The Germans capitalized on this event and fourteen days later German troops landed in

Kiaochow Bay and occupied a village. This eventually resulted in the granting of favorable concessions to Germany. China signed a 99-year lease to Germany of Kiaochow Bay, considered the main port of entry for Manchurian trade. The lease, signed on 5 March 1898, also gave the German empire exclusive rights to build two railways and develop the mines in Shantung province.

With this success, the German government decided to further strengthen her navy. On 28 March 1898, the first Navy Act of Germany was passed by the Reichstag. The Act provided for the expansion of Germany's navy with an appropriation of twenty million Sterling to finance a German fleet of two squadrons composed of nineteen battleships. The fleet was divided into two divisions of eight ships each, two spare ships, and one flagship and around forty large and small cruisers. It was the start of Germany's naval expansion, resulting in her rise as the World's second maritime power during the later part of the 19th century. With this development, she was now ready to protect her colonies and increase German commerce on the high seas. At the same time, it would now be possible to extend her power over underdeveloped countries.

Like other colonialist nations, Germany sought to protect its overseas nationals and trade interests to the extent of safeguarding free access to markets. Her foreign policy was to acquire overseas colonies anywhere and everywhere in the world. At about this time, the momentous Battle of Manila Bay took place on 1 May 1898, following the outbreak of the Spanish-American War. The victory scored by US Commodore George Dewey's fleet brought the Far East, particularly the Philippines, to the attention of the world. Germany was one of those which recognized the great potentialities of the islands as a major commercial market. Germany became interested in the outcome of the war, especially on the destiny of the rich colonies of Spain.

She likewise feared to see the American imperialistic arms extended over the area. The idea of eventual appropriation by the US of Spanish colonies anywhere in the world, particularly in the Far East, was not a good scenario for Germany.

Meanwhile, on 11 May, Prince Henry of Prussia, a brother of the German Emperor, sent a dispatch from Hong Kong. He reported that a German merchant based in Manila told him about the possible success of the Filipino rebellion in the Philippines. In the event of a successful overthrow of the Spanish government, the Filipino leader would be more than willing to place the Spanish colony under the protection of another European power. It was indicated that Germany was a first preference among the Western powers. This information was later confirmed by the German Consul in Manila. He cabled Bulow two days later, stating that the Filipinos were not fighting to change masters but were inclined for an establishment of a Filipino kingdom. He concluded by saying that there is a prospect of offering the throne to a German prince.

Immediately after this, Bulow conferred with the emperor. The idea of acquiring the islands without much effort brought forward the dream of a German Philippines. But there was England. Was she not interested in the islands too? The Emperor, through Bulow, sent Vice-Admiral Otto von Diederichs, who was then refitting his fleet in Nagasaki, Japan, to Manila Bay to report to the German government about the real political situation in the islands, including the Filipinos' true sentiment about Germany and other foreign influences. The German ambassador to England, Count Paul von Hatzfeldt-Wildenberg, was also instructed to make an inquiry as to the plan of the British government for the islands. Likewise, German ambassador to Washington, Teodore von Holleben, was asked to find out discreetly the strength of U.S. public opinion on the issue of American annexation of the Philippines.

Germany's design to acquire the Philippines was now pronounced. On 8 June 1898, a month after the Battle of Manila Bay, Bulow sent a confidential communication to his ambassador in Great Britain giving further instructions on Germany's current colonial policy. With the instructions was a list of names of islands and places in Asia, East and West Africa and the Pacific which the German government was interested to acquire. In West Africa, he mentioned a proposed German naval station in the Canaries or Cape Verde Islands; the use of the island of Fernando Po; and the Volga down to its mouth to serve as a German frontier between Togo land and the Gold Coast colony. Angola, with the southern part of Mossamedes and Benguella, and the whole of Walfish Bay, were also named. In East Africa, Germany was interested to get Zanzibar with Pemba and Zambezi and Shire to act as a southern frontier for a German East Africa. In Asia, the Portuguese Timor, the Sulu archipelago, and at least one of the Philippine islands (Mindanao), were listed. In the Pacific, the German interest was on the Caroline and the Samoan islands.

On 12 June, the day the Philippines declared its independence from Spain, Vice-Admiral Diederichs arrived in Manila Bay aboard the *Kaiserin August*, a first class German cruiser. The number of German war vessels in Philippine waters increased to three. Earlier, on 6 and 9 May, respectively, *Irene* and the *Cormoran* arrived in the bay with a separate instruction from the German government, mainly to protect German nationals in Manila. At this time, six American, three German, two British, one French and one Japanese foreign war vessels were in Manila Bay. Two days later, *Prinzess Wilhelm* appeared in Manila Bay. The arrival of these two war ships made Germany the strongest neutral power in the Philippines. Her five ships could easily defeat Dewey's six small war vessels. This did not only arouse American suspicion of Germany's real intention in the Philippines but also added fire to the growing anti-German feeling sweeping the United States.

In Manila, the situation was critical. Everyday, it was becoming tense. The German's continued disregard of the American blockade in Manila Bay irritated Dewey. As far as Diederichs was concerned there was no blockade because there was no formal announcement made by the Americans. The Germans, furthermore, felt superior over the Americans with their well-equipped five war vessels. For several nights, the German ships were seen leaving and arriving in Manila Bay and during these movements they flashed heavily their searchlights, much to the annoyance of the Americans. In some instances, the Germans would send their boats from ship to ship as if on an inspection mission.

Both countries' war ships almost clashed in Subic Bay. On 7 July, when Aguinaldo's troops were about to complete the occupation of the area, the German ship *Irene*, for 'humanitarian reasons, evacuated the non-combatants and in the process shielded the Spaniards at the Isla Grande. Because of this, Dewey sent his two ships, *USS Raleigh* and *Concord*, to Subic Bay to help the Filipinos in taking the island. The expected clash was prevented when the German *Irene* moved out of the bay before the American vessels arrived. Two days after, *Irene* left the Philippines.

As a result of this incident and previous irritants, Dewey challenged the Germans to a fight. It was said that Dewey angrily told the Germans, 'as we are in for it now, it matters little to us whether we fight Spain or Germany, or the world, and if you desire war, you can have it right here. You need not cable Berlin, nor need me to Washington; you can just have war here and now.' Dewey's strongly worded statement might have been made because by that time, *Charleston*, the first US transport carrying three thousand men, had already arrived in Manila, thereby strengthening his fleet and bringing enough ammunition.

Earlier, before the 13 August surrender of Manila, the different foreign vessels docked in the bay were notified by Dewey about the attack. They positioned themselves in places out of the line of fire. During the 'mock battle of Manila Bay,' the British war vessels, *Immortalite* and *Iphigenia,* reportedly positioned themselves between the US and the German ships. This unpredictable movement of the British ships resulted in the claim that the American ships were saved by the English from German attack. This incident, of course, was dismissed by American historians as purely legend.

Two days later, Diederichs was instructed to go to Batavia, now Jakarta, to take part in the coronation ceremonies in honor of Queen Wilhelmina. The following day, the news about the peace protocol signed in 12 August, reached Manila. Germany's interest in the Philippines was cut short with the signing of the Treaty of Paris on 10 December 1898. The Philippines was finally annexed by the United States in 1899. In a memorandum prepared by Bulow dated 14 March 1899 to Prince Henry of Prussia, commanding officer of the entire German squadron in the Far East, the empire's colonial ambition over the Philippines was relegated to the background of her other interests. The memorandum, prepared to brief the prince on the general political situation affecting US-German relations, stated in part:

'... the Spanish government has handed to us the Caroline, Pellew, and Marianne Islands excluding Guam, in return for the sum of sixteen million Marks and certain trade concessions. We shall thus become neighbors of the Americans who possess the Philippines...

'... A conflict with the great North American republic, whose self-confidence has been greatly increased by the success against Spain, would be very unwelcome to us just now. His Majesty's government therefore earnestly desires to settle the business differences between Germany and the United States in a friendly manner and to clear up the Samoan affair...

'The ships of His Majesty's squadron are the subject of special resentment in the U.S. It is therefore of greatest importance to us that His Majesty's fleet should with careful tact, but naturally preserving its dignity to the full, aim at avoiding any conflict with the American Navy and authorities.

'Also, for the sake of our coming occupation of the Caroline Islands we must be assured against disturbances by the Americans. So we must avoid any appearance of supporting the rebellious *Tagals*, and especially of any intention of extending our influence over the Philippines.'

NHI Photo

Filipinos' Little War with the Americans

More than a century ago, the freedom loving Filipinos went to war against the Americans to protect their country from colonisation. Of course, the Filipinos, who later became known as the 'little brown Americans of Asia', lost the war, but the fact remains that it was a manifestation of the peoples' courage and desire to determine their own destiny.

The signing of the Treaty of Paris on 10 December 1898 between Spain and the United States transferring control over the islands without consultation with the Filipinos resulted in irritants in Filipino-Americans relations. Incidents followed incidents and inevitably led to the outbreak of hostilities. Attempts to relax the growing tension between the two people were made, but failed.

Filipino-American relations turned for the worse when on the night of 4 February 1899, an American sentry, in violation of his superior officer's order, fired upon and killed a Filipino soldier in Sta. Mesa, Manila. The following day, General Arthur MacArthur, father of General Douglas MacArthur of the 'I shall return' fame, issued his order to advance against the Filipino troops.

The Filipino military commanders who were with General Emilio Aguinaldo, the leader of the Filipino revolutionary forces, then in Malolos, Bulacan, attending a dance, were surprised at the turn of events. The rapidity with which the American military units moved that night showed premeditation on the part of the leaders. General Emilio Aguinaldo had no alternative but to issue a call to arms and to advise the people to make more sacrifices for the country.

The Filipino-American War was a one-sided affair, American superiority in arms proved victorious in the bloody encounters that followed in other places north of Manila. Despite this, the Americans suffered some reverses in the field and lost many men and materials. General Elwell Otis, the military leader, predicted that the war would end in a few months. It lasted for three solid years, characterised by Filipinos fighting savagely against great odds.

At the Battle of Quingua, the American cavalry, under General Franklin Bell; suffered a defeat at the hands of General Gregorio del Pilar. Colonel John M. Stotsenberg was killed during the encounter. General Henry Lawton perished at the battle of San Mateo, which was heroically commanded by General Licerio Geronimo. American newspaper correspondents who were covering the conflict praised the tenacity, bravery and heroism of Filipino soldiers. On the other hand, they criticised General Otis' behaviour in censoring their stories on the exact nature of the Filipino resistance to American imperial designs. For two years, the Americans hunted General Aguinaldo like a wounded animal, but the wily Filipino leader, cool as ever, traversed mountains, hills, valleys, and trails and crossed streams in a desperate attempt to elude the pursuing enemy. He finally holed up in the God-forsaken town of Palanan, Isabela Province, on the Pacific side of North eastern Luzon. From there he directed guerrilla operations. However, through treachery and double-cross, General Aguinaldo was captured and brought to Manila, and on 1 April 1901 he took his oath of allegiance to the United States Government. Meanwhile, the American soldiers employed 'humane methods' to make the Filipinos cooperate.

On the island of Samar, an American general, infuriated by the tactics of the Filipino guerrillas, ordered his men 'to kill and burn' and added 'the more you kill and burn the better it will please me.' Samar was transformed into a 'howling wilderness' when even boys above the age of ten were ruthlessly murdered by the Americans. In April 1902, General Miguel Malvar of Batangas laid down his arms, his surrender marking the end of the Filipino-American War.

America's brand of terrorism

The chaos and confusion happening in Iraq today has a similarity to Philippine history. It was a period when America's self proclaimed altruistic goal brought them to Asia, on the pretext of liberating (sound familiar?) and civilising the Filipinos who had been under the spell of Christian dogma and belief three centuries before the Americans came into the picture. It is history repeating itself when Iraq was placed in a similar situation.

The Abu Ghraib and Guantanamo prisons remind one about the reconcentration of Filipinos during the early American military occupation, which, like the infamous prisons, brought shame to America. The American population was shocked after learning, through media corespondents, of the events unfolding, of the real happening in far away Philippines. The damage caused to the Filipinos could almost parallel the Iraqis' experience with the American occupation forces now.

Filipinos' hatred of the Americans was highlighted by the massacre of an entire American infantry in a small village of Balangiga at the southern tip of Samar Island. The village was a peaceful town garrisoned by an U.S. army detachment, but the outside areas under American control were inhabited by Filipinos opposed to the American occupation of the Philippines. Leon Wolff's *Little Brown Brother* tells the story of the massacre that led to the pronouncement by General 'Jake's Smith of those famous words: 'I want no prisoners,' he said. 'I wish you to kill and burn; the more you burn and kill the better it will please me.' He ordered to convert Samar into 'a howling wilderness.' The ensuing events showed that Filipinos who had not surrendered and were capable of carrying arms would be shot. The capability of a Filipino to inflict harm on an American was defined as 'any one boy of ten could carry a rifle and swing a bolo and should be considered as dangerous as their elders.' Major Waller of the Marines was tasked to implement Smith's order without qualms. Within six months, Samar was 'as quiet as a cemetery.'

In Batangas, Filipinos were classified either as active friends or enemies. The enemies, regardless of age and sex, were ordered to be killed or captured and everyone had to live in reconcentration areas. Outside the concentration zones, food was confiscated or destroyed and a curfew enforced by the military. Wolff described the situation in Batangas: "... any Filipino found on the street after that hour was to be shot on sight. Whenever an American soldier was killed, a native prisoner would be chosen by lot and executed. Native houses in the vicinity of telegraph lines cut by the insurrections would be burned.'

Like the modern day Major-General Taguba, James H. Blount, a lieutenant of American volunteers who later became a judge in the Philippines, submitted a report on similar atrocities and abuses as those committed by the present occupation forces in Iraq: 'the American soldier in officially sanctioned wrath is a thing so ugly and dangerous that it would take a Kipling to describe him; and the punitive expedition conducted early in 1902 was a classic of its genre, resulting in the devastation of the countryside and the total extirpation of guerrilla resistance there.'

In the Visayas, by the middle of 1901 Cebu was placed under military control. Historian Resil Mojares, in his book *The War against the Americans: Resistance and Collaboration in Cebu 1899-1906*, said: 'With the return of Cebu to military rule on 17 July 1901, American troops took to the field in earnest. Many of the American sorties at this time were plain killing expeditions. During a four-month period, from July to October 1901, when the insurgent surrenders took place, there were no less than 23 recorded encounters in various parts of the province, resulting in more than 100 Cebuanos killed and around 50 captured....' He also noted that: 'On 1 August 1901, soldiers of the Nineteenth U.S. Infantry, aided by the Argao police, attacked a group of men at a public dance in a barrio near Argao. The revellers were suspected of being insurgents and the Americans proceeded to kill 20 of them. One American soldier and an Argao policeman were wounded. How is that, in comparison to the wedding event in Iraq which was marred by death when American forces swooped on the house where the wedding celebration was being held?

On 2 October 1901, it was reported that men of the Nineteenth U.S. Infantry drove a band of 'bolo men' into a cave near Dumanjug and killed 11 men. The only injuries sustained by the Americans were from stones hurdled at them by the Cebuanos trapped inside the cave. In this kind of encounter, 'prisoners were killed as they reportedly 'tried to escape.' This is similar to some disappearances that have been reported in Iraq.

The maltreatment of Filipinos by the American occupation forces did not only happen among ordinary Filipinos. Known town officials were also subjected to what historians described as the 'water cure.' Cases of military atrocities were reported and three cases were exposed in the newspapers in Cebu. The revelations resulted in a military investigation of three cases involving prominent leaders of the community, four of them Cebu *presidente*. Investigated were the use of the 'water cure' on prisoners, the rape of two women and the maltreatment of a priest and some citizens in Bogo, Cebu.

One such incident involving well-known citizens was about Diego Cabrera and his friend Filomeno Veloso, who were arrested by the Americans in August 1900.

'... around 10 American soldiers forced their way into the house of Diego Cabrera on Calle Gravina because of the information that he owned a gun as a former chief of police. Cabrera, who was ill at the time, was forced to go with the soldiers dressed in nothing but his drawers and undershirt. Also taken to the barracks were Cabrera's houseguest and a cousin. Cabrera was subjected to 'water treatment' until he fell unconscious. The prisoners were released only the following morning when the misunderstanding was finally cleared up ...'

When it was found out that the soldier involved in the case was intoxicated at the time of the arrests. He was reprimanded by higher officers and confined to quarters.

The almost three years of initial occupation of the Philippines is known in history as the Filipino-American War. During that short period of time, 4,234 American soldiers were killed and buried in the Philippines; hundreds more later died in America of service related diseases; 2,818 were wounded, and some were unaccounted for. One may ask, how many Iraqis will die until the Americans leave the oil-rich but troubled country? The aftermath of the war in the Philippines resulted in 16,000 Filipino revolutionaries killed, with 'corpses actually counted by the Americans.' As in Iraq today, bodies disappear in the middle of the night, and so the total estimate in the Philippines was around twenty thousand Filipinos who perished in that period, where the democratic principles were being introduced, and about 200,000 civilians died of pestilence or disease that followed the American pacifications campaign.

What they say about the 'little war'.

'The extraordinary circumstances of the annexation of the Philippine Islands and the bloody three-year war that followed the insurrection of its eight million inhabitants (a war in which almost a quarter of a million US troops and Filipinos died) are today all but forgotten, even in America.' – Leon Wolff, *Little Brown Brother*, 1960.

'Filipinos have never been discouraged by the weakness of their forces, nor have they known fear; courageously they have travelled along the path of rectitude and strength...' - General Emilio Aguinaldo.

'Today at 9pm, the American cannon opened fire upon us, and as they continued in spite of our silence we also began firing.' – Filipino commander Fernando E. Grey.

'We had lent them [Filipinos] guns and ammunition, advised with them; exchanged pleasant courtesies with them; placed our sick and wounded in their kindly care; entrusted our Spanish prisoners to their humane and honest hands; fought shoulder to shoulder with them against the common enemy; praised their gallantry; praised their mercifulness; praised their fine and honourable conduct; borrowed their trenches; borrowed their strong positions which they had previously captured from the Spaniards; petted them; lied to them – officially proclaiming that our land and naval forces came to give them their freedom and displaced the bad Spanish Government – fooled them, used them until we needed them no longer; then derided the sucked orange and threw it away.' – Mark Twain

'The Filipinos are said to be barbarians, incapable of self-government, because it is alleged they are unacquainted with the conventionalities of civilisation. But this is utterly untrue. The Filipinos can govern, and govern well, the people of their islands. Those at the head of the present republic are men of culture, of taste, and of education...'
– Richard Brinsley Sheridan, British author.

WHAT WILL HE DO WITH IT?

4

Brown Americans of Asia

In 48 years, to be exact, under American tutelage, Filipinos have become confused and alienated. They don't know their cultural and historical past. Those who *are* aware, are superficial in depth. They are always in search of their identity; have they neither belonged to the East nor the West.

The more than 300 hundred years of Spanish colonisation resulted in the Filipinos of today who are non-committed in their religious belief. Contemporary Filipinos are very much proud of telling the world around them that they come from the only Christian country in Asia, to emphasise the point that they are different from the rest of their Asian neighbours. The idea of being different was heightened when the Americans came.

During the early part of American colonisation of the Philippines, Carl Crow, an American journalist who was assigned in the Philippines between 1901 and 1905, described the Filipinos as 'our little Brown brother, the Filipino, pure and simple whom we are all so anxious to uplift to his proper place upon earth and relieve from the burdens cast upon him by heredity and a few hundred years of Spanish dominion, is without doubt unreliable, untrustworthy, ignorant, vicious, immoral and lazy.'

The American correspondent continued to describe the Filipino as 'patient and ingenious over small things and he will work for weeks making a simple straw hat but he is tricky and as a race, more dishonest than any known race on the face of the earth.'

The American housewives who followed their spouses to the Philippines after the end of the Filipino-American War provided an interesting portrait on how the Americans saw the people they had 'to liberate from Spanish bondage.' The Colonial American women grouped the Filipinos into two: the distasteful Filipino politicians who brought trouble to their American husbands, and Filipino servants whom they called only by their first names and whose main duty was to provide comfort to the family and, in some cases, entertainment with their 'childlike' qualities. The early Americans in the Philippines suffered from a rare 'disease' in dealing with the Filipinos, their colonial subjects, and this is called Colonial Schizophrenia.

According to Filipino journalist Virginia Benitez-Licuanan, the disease was common to all early Americans who stayed for long periods of time in the tropical Philippines, surrounded by a subjugated brown-skinned people. She added that the disease was very common and most virulent among Americans of low or lower middle class origins. She defined colonial schizophrenia as a heightened sensitivity to the relative degree of skin colour, a sensitivity that swiftly deteriorates into comparing the degree of pigmentation and to consider lack of epidermal tint as some kind of special virtue or quality that supersedes social or intellectual qualities. The colonialists have a delusion of superiority intrinsic in the possession of white skin. Licuanan also stated that the disease is proven to be infectious among the early Americans. However, it was noted that there is an interesting side-effect after long periods of exposure to colonial schizophrenics.

Subjugated dark skinned people, like the Filipinos, develop a sympathetic disorder which also takes the form of sensitivity to the colour of the skin and they also develop the delusion that white skin is an ideal state and their judgment of individuals is affected by the degree of colour of their skin. After a few decades of constant exposure to colonial schizophrenics, Filipinos, the subjugated people also suffer personality deterioration and conflicting emotions which are characterised by the compulsive desire to emulate the Americans. Deterioration of personality of Filipinos during the American experience is gleaned from another of Crow's statement: 'Filipino does not talk as we do of their own superiority, but it is evident that they are not only unwilling to admit that we belong to a superior race, but are inclined to assume that position for themselves.'

It has been said that majority of the American officials who were assigned in the Philippines where from a lower-middle class background. Majority came from small towns in the United States. They had very few notable family or social backgrounds, but by sheer luck, rights of conquest, official position and Caucasian origin, they became the ruling class in the Philippines soon after their arrival. Many of the ruling Americans, with loyal Filipino household servants, found themselves as the new aristocracy, dependent on official position and colour of skin.

Education was one of the priorities of the American administration. Many young Filipinos, called *pensionados*, were sent to America to learn about American-style democracy. They were to observe and experience the American way of life first hand and to take in the atmosphere of a working democracy under real life conditions. As more Filipinos acquired Western education, American colonials started to regard the Filipinos as people having a quick mind, a sense of humour, artistic sense, and poetic imagination, courteous, brave, and generous. Moreover, as one observer said, 'he can balance a tea cup with assurance and precision' and considered 'more useful than the average American at a dinner or an afternoon tea.'

Changes had taken place among Filipinos. The late historian Teodoro A. Agoncillo said that the educational efforts of the

Americans placed the 'native ideas, customs and traditions and even the national identity of the Filipinos in danger of obliteration.' Under the American tutelage, the school curriculum did not have Filipino content. Young Filipinos were taught American songs, American ideals, the lives of American heroes and great men, but not about the heroism of Filipinos they could emulate and draw inspiration from. In fact, the use of the vernacular language was prohibited. By the time the Philippine Commonwealth was inaugurated in 1935, a full generation of Filipinos went through an 'educational system that was intended as tool of pacification.' American influence on the life of the Filipinos is very strong and solid. According to Agoncillo, the Filipinos were 'apt pupils and need not be whipped into line to perform *foreign tricks*. They are naturally imitative and can out-Spanish or out-American a Spaniard or an American.' Thus, the common belief that the Philippines is the only Christian and the most Westernised country in the Orient.

Initially, American goods that flooded the Philippine market were considered luxuries, but after the American experience they became necessities. Anything that is stateside is better and the inferiority of the local products was over emphasised. There is a strong belief that the American standard of living is the best without analysing that it is detrimental to the growth of the Philippines, particularly its industries. Many studies pointed to the Filipinos partially losing their racial heritage because of their American experience. The close family ties are gone and the love of their language and culture has been replaced by the adoration of the American language and culture. Filipinos are neither conversant in English nor in Filipino, the national language. They are more at ease with *Engalog* or *Taglish*, a proof of their language inadequacies.

A colonial mentality has been a problem since many years back and it is still as strong as, say thirty years ago. Filipinos have an extreme liking for things American without regard for their worth. Subconsciously, the phrase 'nothing like America' is in the minds of the average Filipinos, including those who are now settled and naturalised citizens of Australia. The persistence of the Philippines to become the 51st State of America is proof of this subconscious feeling of the little 'brown American.' As a whole, the Filipinos lost their sense of value of their origin.

First democratic Republic of Asia

The transition only took eight months. From a dictatorial form of government, it became revolutionary, and finally a republic, the first organised in Asia. This is how an Asian democratic republic was born more than a hundred years ago.

General and President Emilio Aguinaldo, the leader of the Philippine revolutionary forces, together with higher officials of his government, returned to the country in May 1898 with the blessings and assistance of the Americans, to resume the war against Spain. Upon arrival in Manila, the revolutionary forces were reorganised and vigorously pursued the plan to form a Filipino government. Initially, a Federal type of government was discussed. However, it was decided, that due to the condition at that time, a strong executive arm of the government was needed. A dictatorial government was therefore established by General Aguinaldo on 24 May 1898 and the government issued decrees to implement its regulations. Soon, all orders issued by the Philippine Government prior to the signing of the *Pact of Biyak-na-Bato* of 1897 and all commissions issued to officials of the army, provinces, and towns were declared null and void. General Aguinaldo ordered everyone to observe humanely the laws of war in order to show the world that Filipinos were 'sufficiently civilised and capable of governing themselves.' A severe penalty was prescribed, including death, for crimes of murder, robbery and rape.

The events that developed were unexpected. On 12 June 1898, General Aguinaldo declared Philippine independence from Spanish control. The Philippine national flag and anthem, symbols of Filipino nationhood, were officially unfurled and played to a jubilant crowd. The Dictatorial Government lasted until 23 June 1898, when a Revolutionary Government was established. The government had a simple governmental structure consisting of a President and four departments. There was a Revolutionary Congress composed of provincial representatives. Instead of a judiciary, a permanent commission heard suits from provincial governments and for military justice. By the end of 1898, key officials in the government, including military officers, were already appointed. A significant feature of the revolutionary government was the creation of the Department of Foreign Relations, Navy and Commerce, with the Bureau of Foreign Relations responsible for matters pertaining to diplomatic activities, including diplomatic dispatches and correspondences of the Philippine Republic with foreign governments. A Revolutionary Committee abroad was assigned to negotiate with foreign ministries on the recognition of Philippine independence. In August 1898, the Filipino government published in Hong Kong papers the text of the independence proclamation and a manifesto addressed to foreign governments.

The manifesto explained the true cause of the Philippine revolution and requested various foreign governments to recognise Filipino belligerency and independence. The Aguinaldo government claimed that the Philippines, as a nation, 'has already arrived at the state where it can and should govern itself.' It was during this time that General Aguinaldo reorganised the Hong

Kong Revolutionary Committee composed of a central directorate, members and foreign correspondents or diplomatic agents assigned in France, England, United States, Japan and Australia. The 'diplomatic agents' named were Pedro Roxas and Juan Luna for France; Antonio Ma. Regidor and Sixto Lopez for England; Felipe Agoncillo for the United States; Mariano Ponce and Faustino Lichauco for Japan; and Heriverto Zarcal for Australia.

All efforts, however, to gain foreign recognition for the Republic failed. No favourable response was accorded the *de facto* Filipino government by the leading foreign powers like the United Kingdom, France, Russia, Germany and Japan. The transition from a revolutionary government to a democratic republican form of structure was undertaken through the Philippine Revolutionary Congress, also known as Malolos Congress. The constituent body framed the organic law of the Philippine state.

The Malolos Constitution established a free and independent Republic of the Philippines. It provided for a popular, representative, alternative and responsible government based on the principle of separation of powers - executive, legislative and judiciary. Freedom of religion and the separation of Church and the State were recognised. The rights of citizens and aliens were safeguarded by a Bill of Rights. An elected Assembly of representatives exercised the legislative powers, while a President, elected by the Assembly, performed the executive functions of the government. Judicial power rested in the Supreme Court of Justice and other courts created by law. A Chief Justice appointed by the Assembly and concurred in by the President, headed the judiciary.

A permanent legislative committee acted as legislative body when the Assembly was not in session. Also provided for was: parliamentary immunity; a penal responsibility of high ranking officials for crimes committed against the safety of the State; a

Council of State composed of the President and his secretaries; and a local government and departmental autonomy.

The legislative body ratified the 12 June 1898 Act of Proclamation of Philippine Independence on 29 September 1898. The Malolos Republic became the first democratic republic in Asia. Unfortunately, it was a short-lived republic. It lasted two years and two months, for the Americans successfully destroyed it by force of arms. The Republic was proclaimed on 21 January 1899. It was the embodiment of Filipinos' aspirations to control their destiny. In spite of being branded by the Americans as an ephemeral republic or the paper government of the Filipinos, and dismissed as a mere lesson in patriotism, the First Philippine Republic was a working government with notable leadership headed by President Emilio Aguinaldo and assisted by military officers and a civilian cabinet.

Learning American democracy

One hundred and ten years ago Filipinos declared their independence from Spanish colonial control. It was a short lived freedom. For almost three years, Filipinos fought against the Americans – the new colonial master.

The Filipino-American War ended in 1901 and the Philippines became an American colony. Prior to this event, while the war was raging the Americans established a military government in the Philippine. It was headed by a military governor-general who exercised both executive and legislative powers until 1901.

The military authorities reorganised the judiciary and promulgated a code of criminal procedure, introduced popular elections and political autonomies of municipalities, including the reorganisation of the local governments.

In 1899, the First Philippine Commission, also known as the

Schurman Commission, arrived in the Philippines. Subsequently, a recommendation as to what type of government appropriate for the Filipinos was submitted. A civilian government with a bicameral legislature and a system of public education were favoured. The Commission also recommended the conservation of the islands' natural resources; organisation of municipal and provincial governments, and the appointment of Filipinos to important government offices.

The Republic of Negros was the only experience of the Filipinos in dealing with local government administration. It was a premature attempt by the Americans to establish a civil government in the island of Negros in 1899. A constitutional convention was held and framed the constitution of a Negros republic. The constitution was patterned after state governments of the American union. The first election under the Negros Constitution was held on 2 October 1899. The Republic of Negros was dismantled when it became a regular province under the local government system established by the Americans in 1901.

A Second Philippine Commission, also known as the Taft Commission, was sent to the Philippines by the American government in 1900 to take charge of the transfer of government administration from the military to civilian authorities. The Taft Commission exercised legislative and executive powers. For two years, it enacted more than four hundred laws, including the creation of the Civil Service System, establishment of municipal and provincial governments, organised the Philippine Constabulary, created the first Insular Bureau of Agriculture and Industry, provided a public school system, and created the local government of Benguet.

In 1902, US President Theodore Roosevelt approved the Philippine Bill of 1902. The Philippine Assembly was created and granted the responsibility of sharing legislative functions throughout the colony, except areas inhabited by the Moros and Non-Christian. The law provided the Filipinos their first lessons in lawmaking, for the Philippine Assembly functioned as the lower house of the Legislature and the Taft Commission, the upper house. When it was convened on 17 October 1907, it was wholly composed of Filipinos. Former Cebu Governor Sergio Osmeña and the former Tayabas (now Quezon province) Governor, Manuel L. Quezon, were elected as speaker and majority floor leader, respectively. Two Filipino resident commissioners in Washington were also authorised to represent Filipino interests in the US Congress, but did not have the right to vote. The Philippine Autonomy Act, also known as the Jones Law, was passed by the US Congress in 1916. It was the first formal American commitment to recognise the Independence of the Philippines, initially declared in 1898.

A bicameral legislature composed of a House of Representatives with eighty nine members and a Philippine Senate with twenty four members was established. Members of the Legislature were elected according to representative and senatorial districts, except for the representatives and senators of non-Christian provinces, who were appointed by the governor-general.

Senator Manuel L. Quezon and Representative Sergio Osmeña were elected President of the Senate and Speaker of the House of Representatives, respectively. The Legislature exercised general legislation functions, except on subjects pertaining to coinage, currency, immigration or tariffs, including those related to lands of public domain, timber and mining, which still required the approval of the US President.

The Jones Law represented a new era in the democratic processes in the Philippines. It suited the growing nationalist orientation of the members of the Philippine Assembly. The Legislature played an active part in running the government. It was a 'quasi-parliamentary form of government dominated by Osmeña and Quezon,' according to Filipino historian Teodoro A. Agoncillo.

The Legislative body's last act was the framing and adoption of the 1935 Philippine Constitution and the establishment of the Commonwealth of the Philippines. The country was on the road to recapture the lost political independence of 1898.

In 1934, the population elected 202 delegates to the Constitutional Convention. Senator Claro M. Recto, a nationalist, was elected President of the Convention, with senators Ruperto Montinola and Teodoro Sandiko serving as the first and second vice-presidents. Narciso Pimentel was the convention secretary. For many years, the 1935 Constitution was influenced by committee reports, the Biak-na-Bato and the Malolos Constitutions, McKinley's 'instruction' to the Second Philippine Commission, the Philippine Bill of 1902 (Cooper Act) and the Philippine Autonomy Act of 1916. It was also influenced in parts by the constitutions of the United States, Germany, Italy, Poland, Mexico, Spain and some Latin American Countries.

A presidential form of government was provided for in the Constitution, with a unicameral lawmaking body known as the National Assembly. Other major functions of the government included executive powers, judicial, electoral and constituent functions. The Commonwealth government was inaugurated on 15 November 1935. The first law passed by the national assembly was the National Defence Act. Other important laws were the Court of Industrial Relations Act in 1936, the Minimum Wage Act, the Tenancy Act, the Public Defence Act, and the Education Act of 1940. In 1940, the National Assembly approved the amendments of the Constitution, changing the tenure of office of the President and Vice-President of the Philippines from six years without re-election to four years with re-election. Re-adoption of a bicameral legislature and the creation of the Commission on Elections also took place.

The Fall of Corregidor on 6 May 1942 ended the organised resistance against the Japanese invasion. As a result, President Quezon carried on with the Commonwealth Government operations from Washington D.C. until 1944. On 29 June 1944, US Congress voted for the recognition of the Independence of the Philippines and set the date for 4 July 1946. Although the 1898 independence of the Philippines was recognised, Filipinos were deprived of celebrating it until the early 1960s when the Independence Day celebration was changed from 4 July to 12 June every year.

For the last thirty three years, the Filipinos have been celebrating that glorious day when the population decided to declare their independence from colonial control.

Australia: Sanctuary to a Filipino president

Contrary to the claim in the Filipino community that the arrival of President Fidel V. Ramos in Sydney several years ago was 'the first visit of a Philippine President to Australia', newspapers during the war years recorded the visit to Australia of Philippine President Manuel L. Quezon, where he officially broadcast a message to the Filipinos fighting the Japanese.

Official diplomatic relations between the Philippines started in 1946 when President Manuel A. Roxas was sworn in as President of the Republic of the Philippines. Prior to this, diplomatic relations of the Philippines with foreign countries, including Australia, were conducted through the Department of State of the United States government, thePhilippines being an American colony.

This arrangement continued even when the Commonwealth Government was inaugurated in 1935, with Manuel L. Quezon as president and Sergio Osmeña as vice-president. President Quezon was re-elected in 1941, a few weeks before the outbreak of the Second World War. When the war broke out, President Quezon was in Baguio with his daughter, Baby, while his wife, Aurora Aragon Quezon, was in Pampanga with her son and Jovita Fuentes, the Filipino opera singer. The Quezons immediately returned to Manila and stayed at their Marikina estate. When the news of the arrival of the Japanese in Manila was confirmed, the Quezon family, with Vice-president Sergio Osmeña, Chief Justice of the Supreme Court Jose Abad Santos, Major General Basilio J. Valdes, Colonel Manuel Nieto and his private secretary, Serapio D. Canceran were evacuated to Corregidor. Dr. Andreas Trepp, a lung specialist attending President Quezon, also joined the group.

Their stay in Corregidor was not good for President Quezon whose fragile health was rapidly deteriorating. Upon advice from General Douglas MacArthur, Dr. Trepp and General Valdes, the Quezon government and family boarded the submarine *Swordfish* for the Visayas, and then proceeded to Mindanao. At midnight of 19 February 1942, they were flown to Australia on a B-17 Flying Fortress. Except for Mrs. Quezon, none of the Quezon family had travelled by plane before. President Manuel Quezon of the Philippines arrived in Melbourne by train from Adelaide in the later part of March 1942. He was accompanied by his wife and family and three members of his Cabinet. The Filipino guests were on board a special two coach train when they arrived at the Spencer Street station in Melbourne.

The party was greeted by General Douglas MacArthur and Mrs. MacArthur. Also in the welcoming party were Major-General R. K. Sutherland, Brig-Gen. R. J. Marshall, Col. C. A. Willoughby, Col. S. Hull, Col. Le Grande Diller, Capt. J. R.

McMicking, and Australian and Filipino friends.

Many people crowded around to get a glimpse of the famous President, who, as ruler of the Philippines, is said to have possessed more power than Franklin D. Roosevelt had yet dreamed of. Beside the tall General MacArthur, President Quezon looked small and frail; however, he survived the difficult travel from the Philippines. A city newspaper described him as 'short, slim and swarthy, with grey hair and penetrating eyes.' The ailing 64 year old Filipino head of state was obviously tired after the long and perilous journey. This was the reason why President Quezon, who is known for his public speaking prowess in any of the three official languages of the Philippines - English, Spanish, or Tagalog – did not have a press conference or interview upon arrival in Melbourne. The entourage went from the station to a suburban home that was made available to them. In the afternoon he spent long sessions with General MacArthur. News circulated that President Quezon would remain and make Australia his headquarters to carry on the operation of the Philippine government.

It was while in Melbourne that President Quezon officially informed the Filipinos about the reason of his departure. Quezon's address said:

> 'To the Filipino people and the Philippine Army: At the request of General MacArthur I have left the Philippines and joined him at his headquarters in Australia. On previous occasions suggestions have been made to me that I leave the Philippines, but I refused to do so, determined as I was to carry on with the affairs of government in Philippine territory.
> 'Upon the appointment of General MacArthur to command the Allied forces in this part of the world he invited me to join him, on the ground that we could continue, as we have done in the past, to co-operate better if we were together than if we were separated, with the difficulties in the means of communication.
> 'Having no other objective in mind than to free the Philippines,

I did not hesitate to accept the suggestion of General MacArthur despite the hazards that the trip involved. And so I am here where I expect to be ableto be of assistance in the re-conquest of every foot of territory of our beloved country. 'It is my hope that the results of the appointment of General MacArthur to the High Command and my having followed his advice to join him will soon be felt in the Philippines. I call upon every Filipino to keep his courage and fortitude and to have faith in the ultimate victory of our cause.'

President Quezon and his family and members of his cabinet stayed in Australia until a few days after the fall of Bataan. They boarded the *President Coolidge* on their way to the United States. The Quezon group stayed at the Shoreham Hotel in Washington D.C.

Was July 4 a grant of Filipino independence?

For sixteen years, Filipinos celebrated their independence day on a wrong date – 4 July. To Filipino-Australians who are aware of their original country's history, it was an error that was perpetuated by Filipino leadership schooled under American tutelage. As a consequence, Filipinos were denied the opportunity to commemorate a significant event in their lives – the assertion of their freedom from colonial bondage.

On 12 June 1898, General Emilio Aguinaldo proclaimed Philippine independence from Spanish control. It was followed by the inauguration of the First Philippine Republic early the following year. The next couple of years were difficult for the fledgling republic, the first democratic republic organised in Asia. Many Filipinos fought the new colonial masters and died defending their freedom. This was the Filipino-American War. It ended in 1901 when General Aguinaldo was captured, followed by the surrender of General Miguel Malvar, the last revolutionary leader, the following year.

On 4 July 1902, US President Theodore Roosevelt proclaimed the end of the war in the Philippines and that 'peace returned' to the islands. The period that followed was characterised by suppression of nationalist feeling of the Filipinos. The campaign to regain the independence proclaimed in 1898 was hard and slow. However, the independence campaign received nationwide support and finally a semi-independent Commonwealth was established.

The problem faced by the Filipinos in regaining their 1898 independence was compounded by the outbreak of the Second World War. When the Japanese were driven out of the Philippines and the war years were over, the Americans did not have any alternative except to withdraw American sovereignty over the Philippines. This was in 1946. In an official proclamation, US President Harry S. Truman stated:

> '... the United States of America hereby withdraws and surrenders all rights of possession, supervision, jurisdiction, control or sovereignty now existing and exercised by the United States of America in and over the territory and people of the Philippines.'

Speaking for his country, the American chief executive added that 'I do hereby recognise the independence of the Philippines as a separate and self-governing nation.' The proclamation was clear that it was recognition and not a declaration of independence. By the time the Americans recognised Philippine independence initially declared in 1898, many Filipinos were already conditioned to the American ways of doing things, including the celebration of America's Independence Day, which is also on 4 July.

The Americanization of the Filipinos was so effective, that even today the character of the 'little brown Americans' of Asia lingers on. People got used to commemorating the birth of their freedom on a wrong date. The feeling of Filipino nationhood was therefore not realised, for every year, on 4 July, the celebration of Philippine Independence Day coincided with the Americans 'declaration of independence. It was overwhelmed and overshadowed in all respects by the American Independence Day anniversary. Many observers considered the Filipino celebration of 4 July as a manifestation of their subservience to the United States.

Consequently, the significance of the 1898 Independence proclamation was relegated to the background, while the whole country commemorated their independence day on the fourth of July. However, early in 1960, the Philippine Historical Association (PHA) petitioned the President and the Congress of the Philippines to adopt and declare 12 June every year as the true independence day of the country.

Arguments became heated and nasty. The issue approximates the republican issue of contemporary Australia. The American colonial bond was strong. American educated Senator Camilo Osias was one of those who opposed the change, but in the end found the light and strongly supported the PHA position. According to Historian Esteban A. de Ocampo, the 12 June proclamation was desirable for it was an act undertaken by Filipinos themselves in the exercise of their 'voluntary, spontaneous, deliberate, solemn and sovereign will.'

Commenting on the same subject, Senator Ambrosio Padilla stated during the debate that the Truman Proclamation was a 'notorious document in international law for proclaiming the independence of the Philippines when by tradition and by history the only ones that can proclaim the independence of a country are the people of that country.' More Filipinos were enlightened and believed that it was appropriate to rectify the practice of observing and celebrating their independence day on 4 July of every year.

The PHA, however, did not dismiss the importance of 4 July in Philippine history. The learned body recommended that the date be commemorated instead as a thanksgiving day for the restoration and recognition of Philippine independence by the Americans. It was a national issue that found support from the then President Diosdado Macapagal, who, in 1962, issued a proclamation declaring 12 June, instead of 4 July, as Philippine Independence Day. In issuing the presidential directive, President Macapagal stated that the heroic and inspiring event was a legitimate assertion by the Filipinos of their natural and inalienable claim to freedom and independence. He added that that the date should be observed with fitting ceremonies that will inspire Filipinos to greater dedication for the country. Macapagal's proclamation was confirmed in 1964 by the Congress of the Philippines when it enacted legislation changing the date of Philippine Independence Day from 4 July to 12 June, and declaring 4 July as Philippine Republic day.

Philippine President Manuel A. Roxas being congratulated by General Douglas MacArthur during the 4 July inauguration. NHI Photo

5

First Filipino diplomatic mission

The Tydings Mcduffie Act the United States provided the Filipinos with a ten year transition period (1935-1946) to prepare themselves for self-government. Civil servants were trained to gain experience in practically every branch of governmental functions, except in the field of Foreign Service, which was then handled by the United States.

As Filipino leaders were gaining experience in running their own affairs, the Second World War intervened. After the war, the Philippines became one of the most devastated countries in Asia. The economy was in total ruin and the situation was compounded by the menacing Huk rebellion. Filipinos were pauperised and demoralised. Total rehabilitation and reconstruction was needed for the country to stand on its feet. The transition period could have been extended, but the United States was determined to fulfil its promise to grant the recognition of independence in 1946.

Although late, there was an effort on the part of Filipino leaders to prepare young men and women for the task of international relations. In September 1945, the Commonwealth government created the Office of Foreign Relations to recruit and train Filipinos in diplomatic and consular work. Prospective Filipino foreign affairs officers received instruction in the US Department of State Foreign Service Officers Training School.

Another law was passed creating a Department of Foreign Affairs to take effect on 4 July 1946.

Official diplomatic relations between Australia and the Philippines started in 1946 when the Philippines regained its independence from foreign control, although during the short-lived First Philippine Republic, President Emilio Aguinaldo designated Heriverto Zarcal, a Filipino merchant residing in Queensland, as the government's diplomatic agent in Australia during the period 1898-1901. During the subsequent American occupation of the Philippines, including the Commonwealth period (1936-1943), foreign relations of the Philippines were handled by the United States government.

A new nation was born at the inauguration of the 1946 Philippine government, held at the Luneta, now Rizal Park, with representatives from twenty-three nations in attendance. The United States had the largest delegation. Australia was represented by Commodore Collins of the Royal Australian Navy. In his message to the Philippine government, Australian Prime Minister Ben Chifley, as read by Commodore Collins, recalled the friendship between the two countries that was forged during the last war. The message added that 'as free people, Australia and the Philippines willingly cooperated in a joint effort to achieve a better world.'

Eighteen months later after that ceremony or late in 1947, the first Philippine diplomatic office in Australia was decided by the Department of Foreign Affairs when Executive Order No. 18, 1946 was issued creating the Philippine Foreign Service. The first Consul-General assigned in Sydney was Manuel A. Alzate, who organised the first Philippine diplomatic office in Australia assisted by eight members of his staff.

Consul Alzate was a self-made man who started serving the government at the age of nineteen years old as a rank-and-file and rose to the position of assistant director of the Bureau of Prisons by sheer merit and personal qualifications. He was also regarded as an Orientalist, assemblyman from Nueva Ecija, and lawyer.

A 1920 short biography of him noted that he 'stands head and shoulders over most of the members of the National Assembly in importance, rank, influence, and popularity. He was also known for his competent leadership in public affairs. In fact, he was a member of the *Free Press Honour Roll of the National Assembly.*

Alzate was born on 1 January 1894 in Cervantes, former capital of Lepanto-Bontoc, notably known as the Igorot provinces. In fact, his father, Capitan Ysmael Alzate, 21 years Gobernadorsillo of Bucay, Abra, was an Igorot tribesman who married Maria Dolores Austria, a Spanish mestiza. According to Artigas' *Galeria de Filipinos Ilustres (Gallery of Illustrious Filipinos)*, the elder Alzate rendered a valuable service to the Spanish government in relations to the pacification of the mountain tribes of the Cordillera Central. Because of his service to the Spanish government he was decorated with the medal of '*Merito Civil*' and the '*Cruz Blanca de Primera Clase de Merito Militar.*' He was reported to 'read Latin and speak seventeen languages and dialects including English'. Capitan Alzate was knighted and received the title of '*Caballero de Carlos III.*'

The young Alzate learned his early education from his parents and went to High School in Bangued, Abra, until 1910, at which time he enrolled for his four year commerce course at the Philippine School of Commerce in Manila. After graduation, he worked with the government while continuing his studies in the evening at the College of Law of the National University, where he obtained his LL.B.

In 1918, he was appointed assistant chief clerk of the Bureau of Lands, and the following year was promoted chief clerk. In 1920 he was transferred to the Bureau of Prisons as chief clerk, and four years later became the assistant director of the Bureau of Prisons. He was admitted to the Bar of the Philippines in 1921. In 1923, he represented the Philippines at the Olympic Games held in Japan and travelled to China. He also visited the United States, England, France, Germany and Spain.

In 1925, he was appointed as the official delegate of the Philippine Government to the 9th International Prison Congress in London. He was also commissioned to study *Prison Administration and Organisation of Juvenile Courts in the United States and in Europe* during this trip. At the conference, he delivered a paper entitled *Convict Labor of the Philippine Islands,* which was well received. He became one of the few delegates to travel as a guest of the British government visiting correctional and penal institutions in England and Scotland. During the official dinner given at Aberdeen in honour of the delegates to the conference, William F. Penn, one of the delegates appointed by US President John Calvin Coolidge, congratulated him and said: 'Mr. Alzate, I am proud of the Philippines if you are a representative of the race'.

Mr. Alzate's performance at the conference was also noticed by Commissioner B. Ogden Chisholm of the US International Prisoner Commission, who wrote Governor General Leonard Wood and said: 'I want to thank you for the interest you displayed at this event, and to express my appreciation of your appointment of Mr. Manuel A. Alzate. Mr. Alzate made a very wonderful representative of the Philippine islands. The scope of his knowledge on prisons and statistics was unbounded, and we were very proud to have the Philippine Islands represented by such an able man.' While in the United States, in 1925, he secured an authority to practice law in the Court of Appeals of the District of Columbia and in the Supreme Court of the United States.

His interest on penology continued and he wrote two books: *Convict Labor in the Philippine Islands* in 1925, and *Penal Measures*, a voluminous report on prison systems and legislative enactments and means devised for the repression and prevention of crime, in 1926. His study on the subject brought him recognition from the Graphic Section *Who's Who in the Philippines* in 1932, which asserted that 'there is no doubt that Mr. Alzate is the best informed man in the country today so far as prison problems are concerned.'

During the first National Assembly of the Commonwealth of the Philippines, Mr. Alzate became a member for the first district of Nueva Ecija and chaired the Committee on Foreign Relations. He was also a member of the Committee on Banks and Corporations. He was re-elected to the Philippine legislature in 1938. Equipped with these experiences and qualifications, Mr. Alzate was appointed the first consul general of the Philippines in Sydney. He arrived in Sydney on 14 April 1948. His assistant was Vice-Consul Alejandro Yangko, who was granted provisional recognition by Australia, followed the following month. Alzate, with his family, took temporary residence at 6 Birtley Place, Elizabeth Bay. He organised the first Filipino consular office Down Under with the postal address as GPO 4607. He was assisted by Consul Emilio Bejasa whose appointment was approved by the Australian government in June of the same year. The consular office was given the task of developing trade between the two countries.

The initial year of the infant diplomatic post in Sydney was a difficult one. Aside from solving the problems associated with the search for a suitable place for the office and accommodation for its staff and planning a trade strategy, the consulate was dragged into the controversy surrounding the Gamboa case and which even threatened the closure of the four year old Philippine Consulate General in Sydney. In fighting mood, the members of the House of Representatives voted to delete the £11,000 allocation for the operation of the consular office in Sydney, thereby effectively severing diplomatic relations between the two countries, all because of the White Australia Policy.

Philippine-born US soldier Sargeant Lorenzo Gamboa was refused a visa by Minister Arthur Calwell to visit his Australian wife, Joyce Gamboa, and two children, Julie and Raymond, who were living in Melbourne. In a press interview, Sgt. Gamboa, in desperation, told the United Press about his plan to take his case to the United Nations organization. He was quoted to have said that he planned to go straight to New York after the expiration of his tour of duty in Japan in August 1949. He planned to talk to American First lady Eleonor Roosevelt and General Carlos P. Romulo, the Philippine delegate to the UNO, to raise the question on whether the White Australia Policy was a violation of the UNO Charter. A statement made by Minister Calwell to the media fired Sgt. Gambia's determination. The minister said that he suspected Sgt. Gamboa's plan of visit to Melbourne to see his family was a ploy and his real intention was to enter Australia permanently, with the help of some American military officials in Tokyo.

The decision to bar Sgt. Gamboa from entering Australia brought hard hitting attack from the members of the Philippines Congress. The newly independent lawmakers decided to pass a resolution protesting against Australia's exclusion of Asiatic immigrants. The measure called for the House to express its 'profound and vigorous opposition to Philippine participation in the [Olympic] Games' scheduled in Melbourne in 1956 because of Australia's immigration policy.

Manila newspapers took notice of the incident in Sydney. *The Manila Times*, in particular, observed: 'This is no longer a question of citizenship or race or anything but common decency – a quality in which the Australian immigration policy or its current interpretation seems somewhat deficient.' Another newspaper, *The Evening Chronicle,* rejoined the argument and said: 'If the Australians are being sadistic in this case of Sargeant Gamboa, we cannot entirely blame them. It is the natural sadism that springs from their penal origins.' The insult continued and stated: 'Had they acted otherwise, they would be untrue to the classic traditions of beachcombers newly raised from the gutter.'

Filipino lawmakers in Manila were offended by the refusal and motions were submitted to Philippine Congress to limit foreign entry into the country of nationals of countries not friendly to Filipinos and recommended to close the young Philippine Consulate-General in Sydney. The resolution regarded Australia's racial discrimination policy as a great offence against the Filipino people. Filipino hatred spread to the streets of Manila. Unverified reports of Australians being attacked in the streets of Manila added to the rift between the two countries. There was an initial Filipino campaign for Asians to boycott the Olympic Games scheduled in Melbourne in 1956, and cancellation of aviation talks set in Canberra, all because of the Gamboa case, and this compounded the tense situation in Sydney. *The Sydney Morning Herald* reported the incidents of attack on two Australian officers from steamer *Nellore* in Port Area in Manila.

As the issue heated up in the legislature, Rep. Juan Rodriquez was reported to have said: 'It would be foolish to continue relations with a country advocating racial discrimination.' Because of this action, Philippine Consul-General Manuel Alzate was besieged by the media and asked him to confirm the plan of the Philippine government to close the consulate because of the

Gamboa case. Poor Consul General Alzate, who was not consulted by the lawmakers, obviously denied the news and told the media: 'I have no comment to make. All I know is what I have read in the [Sydney] newspapers.'

However, Immigration Minister Arthur Calwell, who was supported by Prime Minister Chifley, was adamant in his decision to bar Gamboa from entering the country, even as a temporary visitor to see his family, whom he had not seen for more than five years.

The issue continued to attract media interest in Manila, particularly when the Philippine Senate unanimously passed a *Reciprocal Rights Immigration Bill,* as retaliation against the Australian government's refusal to allow Sgt. Lorenzo Gamboa to return to Australia to visit his family. The bill prohibited the admission of aliens [into the Philippines] whose countries do not grant reciprocal rights to Filipinos.' The decision made in Manila was a headline in the *Courier Mail* in Brisbane with a big, bold news banner: '*Philippines Ban on Australian Visitors.*'

Meanwhile, Consul-General Alzate was trying his best to be diplomatic about the whole issue, particularly when Sydney newspapers published the supposed instruction from the Manila Foreign Office ordering all consulates to refuse the grant of visa to Australians who wish to visit the Philippines.

It was in this condition that the Philippines decided to strengthen its consular post in Australia and extended it to New Zealand. The Department of Foreign Affairs, in Manila, announced in July 1949 the promotion and transfer of Philippine Consul-General Alzate to Honolulu to look after the welfare of several thousands of Filipino laborers residing in the islands. Consul-General Roberto Regala, the first consul-general assigned in San Francisco, California, was named as Alzate's successor.

Mr. Regala arrived in Sydney on 14 November 1949 and a

week later his assistant, Consul Tiburcio Baja, arrived. Considered as one of the pioneers in Philippine diplomacy, Hon. Roberto Regala, who retired from public service as ambassador and associate justice of the Supreme Court of the Philippines, found himself in mid-1949 with a new challenge. With energy and spirit, then Consul-General Regala accepted the new post and looked forward to a fruitful tenure in Australia.

He would be appointed to a new diplomatic post, as head of the Philippine diplomatic mission in Sydney, one of the earliest diplomatic offices established by the Philippine government after its 1946 inauguration as an independent nation. It would show to the world that foreign affairs, previously handled by the United States of America, were being given paramount importance by the newly installed Roxas government.

Regala was a seasoned diplomat. He was born on 7 June 1897 in Bacolor, Pampanga. He graduated his Bachelor of Arts degree from the University of the Philippines in 1920. Later he received from the same university his degrees in Science and Government and a Bachelor of Laws, the only UP graduate in that year awarded two degrees in the same academic year.

The following year, he went to the United States and pursued his Doctor of Science in Law at Yale University, and at the same time took special studies in International Law and Constitutional Law at the University of Chicago as well as at Oxford University in England, the Sorbonne University in France, between 1925 and 1926.

After completing his first degree in 1920, he worked with the National Library and Museum as a researcher. It was during this period that he was sent to the United States as a *pensionado* to learn about American-style democracy. He was one of the many young Filipinos who went to America to observe and experience the American way of life first hand and to take in the atmosphere of a working democracy under real life conditions.

He returned to public service as technical assistant in the Department of Interior and later he moved to the Public Service Commission where he stayed until 1932. In 1933 he became a special attorney in the Bureau of Justice and soon after as chief of the legal Research Division of the Department of Justice.

Prior to this position, for a brief period, he was the acting chief of the Division of Foreign Relations in the Office of the President of the Philippines. The unit was the main link of the Philippine Commonwealth Government with the US State Department which handled Philippine foreign affairs, defense and finance. The unit was tasked with preparing Filipinos for diplomatic work in anticipation of the expiration of the ten year transition period at which time Philippine independence would be recognized by the Americans.

It was an informal diplomacy attempted to safeguard the interests of the Philippines and its people. Regala was always busy, but who still found time to teach international and constitutional laws at the University of the Philippines after office hours straight from his government job.

When Philippine independence was finally regained and the government was reconstituted in 1946, Regala became the first legal counselor of the Department of Foreign Affairs, and a few months later he was appointed the first Philippine consul-general at San Francisco, California. He stayed in this post until 1949, at which time he was recalled to the home office. His next posting was Australia as head of the diplomatic office in Sydney. He was elevated to the rank of a Minister.

Minister Regala arrived in Sydney with his wife and three children, on 15 November 1949 to take up his new diplomatic assignment. It was during his stint in Sydney that the Philippine government purchased the present residence of the Philippine

Consul-General in Potts Point for use as the diplomatic office.

Early in 1950, the Philippine Consulate-General's office for Australia and New Zealand was raised to the status of a Legation. It was a reciprocal arrangement by which the Australian government also elevated its consular representation in Manila to the status of a Legation. As a Legation, the ministers of both Legations were assigned additional duties related to political matters. Rear-Admiral George Dunbar Moore became the first Australian Minister to the Philippines. He served this post until his retirement in 1955.

Minister Regala tried his best to correct the imbalance of trade between the Philippines and Australia which was seven to one in favor of the latter. He tried to attract local business companies to the Philippine government's policy of 'tax-free for four years' arrangement for companies investing in the country, but he received a lukewarm response. A Sydney based purchasing agent was even making newspaper interviews stating that there was a 50-million dollars a year market in the Philippines for Australian goods which included flour, dairy products, textiles, leather, tinned corned beef, jam, cattle, horses, and brood mares. And in return, Australia could import timber and tung oil, considered of high quality compared with linseed oil, from the Philippines.

One of the important strategies implemented by Minister Regala, with the blessings of the Manila Foreign Office, was to work for a Philippine-Australia Treaty of Friendship. In fact, he was confident and did not expect difficulty in negotiating the treaty because of the improved friendly relations between Australia and the Philippines. Minister Regala made an appointment with the Comptroller-General of the Department of Trade and Customs for a possible barter trade agreement in which the Philippines would export timber to Australia in exchange for Australian dairy products and beef. He was so determined in his pursuit of his objectives in Sydney that Richard Gardiner (Lord) Casey, who was the Minister for External Affairs of Australia at that time, was irritated by his persistence. In an entry in his diary for 8 August 1952, Lord Casey wrote: 'Regala is knocking hard on our door with proposals for a Treaty of Friendship, etc., with Australia. We have never entered into a Treaty of this sort, and I don't think we can enter into this one.'

Regala however continued in pursuing his diplomatic task to the best of his abilities and experience with organized dialogues with Australian businessmen. He took every opportunity to project the attraction of the Philippines for business interests. But the situation did not change as expected. In desperation, he made it known to Australians that he was serious in his offer. A local newspaper quoted his strong words warning the business community in Australia that the Philippines could no longer make big purchases unless Australia bought more in exchange.

A major event took place during his term of office. It was during his time in Sydney that the bilateral economic and technical assistance among Commonwealth and Non-Commonwealth nations was inaugurated. The agreement later became the famous Colombo Plan. Nation members were both donors and recipients of technical assistance.

On 24 December 1954, the diplomatic rank of Minister Regala was raised to the personal rank of Ambassador by Philippine President Ramon Magsaysay. In January 1956, Ambassador Regala presented his credentials as the first Philippine Ambassador to Australia to the Governor-General, Field Marshal Sir William Slim at the Government House. Seven months later, on 29 august 1956, he left Australia to become the first Philippine Ambassador to Italy. He was replaced by Ambassador Jose F. Imperial. After seven years in Australia, he boarded the plane back to Manila for further instructions from the Manila Foreign Office.

As Philippine ambassador to Italy, he was the concurrent minister to Austria and Israel until 1962, when he was appointed Associate Justice of the Supreme Court during the Macapagal Administration. He reached the compulsory retirement age of 70 in 1967.

During his career, he published numerous books such as *The Development of Representation in the Philippines; Cases and Other Materials in International Law; Bar Questions and Answers in International Law; Public Service Law, Annotated; The Trends in Modern Diplomatic Practices; An Asian Diplomat Looks at the World Today; World Peace Through Law and Diplomacy; Law and Diplomacy in a Changing World; New Dimensions in International Affairs; World Order and Diplomacy;* and *Perspectives in Constitutional Development.*

His achievements in diplomacy were recognized when he was awarded the decoration of The Order of Kalantiaw (First Class) by President Ferdinand Marcos in 1967. Other awards accorded him include the Grand Cordon of the Order of the Brilliant Star by the National Government of the Republic of China and the Grand Cross of Merit by the Italian Government in 1962; Grand Band of Human Order of African Redemption by the President of Liberia in 1960; Grand Cross of St. Sylvestre by Pope John XXIII in 1958; and in 1948 the American International Academy Cross of Academic Honor, Washington, D.C. for his contributions in international law.

His membership with international organizations included the American Society of International Law, Washington, D.C., USA; Victoria Institute of International Law, Madrid, Spain;

Italian Branch, International Commission of Jurists, Rome, Italy; International Institute for Juridical Studies, Rome, Italy; International Law Association, London Branch, England; and Austrian Society of Foreign Affairs and International Relations, Vienna, Austria.

Ambassador Regala served under all the presidents of the Philippines during his active public service life, from President Manuel Roxas to the administration of President Ferdinand E. Marcos. After his retirement in 1967, he continued serving his country as a member of the National Research Council of the Philippines; Department of Foreign Affairs adviser on Law and Diplomacy; a member of a Committee assigned to make a thorough study of existing laws, rules and regulations relative to election laws and registration procedures. He was also designated by President Marcos in 1968 to be the chairman of the Philippine delegation to the UN Conference on the Law of Treaties in Vienna, Austria and became one of the vice-presidents of the said conference.

Consul General Manuel A. Alzate   **Ambassador Roberto Regala** TNL Photos

6

The Stolen generation

Filipinos who have studied the life and works of Jose Rizal, the national hero of the Philippines, will always remember what Rizal said in one of his numerous political and historical writings: 'To foretell the destiny of a nation it is necessary to open the book that tells of her past.' But, unlike Australians, Filipinos do not understand their colorful past, otherwise they would not repeat the same mistakes over and over again. As migrants who settled in this country for a better life and opportunity, Filipinos should show interest in history, not just for their own sake, but for the interests of their young children who would be growing up with a new wave of hopefully changed and enlightened Australians, who are aware of their past, although some are selective in their recollection.

The arrival of the Europeans in Asia and the Pacific during the early part of the 16th century ushered in a new era for the people in this part of the world. Westerners brought with them distinctly new ways of living, believing, creating, and relating to each other. The face of Asia and the Pacific, particularly in its economy, society, culture and people, was forever transformed. Untold stories of displaced 'native' populations became re-current issues. The sufferings of the original inhabitants of these lands have been recorded and become part of peoples' dark colonial past that continues to haunt their national psyche.

The story of the stolen generation of Australia is one of those dreadful consequences of colonial occupation of distant lands. Until recently, the controversy surrounding the stolen generation continued to affect relations between the Australian government and the descendants of the original inhabitants of this country.

Like racism, the issue will not fade away, no matter what strategy the government adopts in the name of reconciliation. It has been written in the colonial history of Australia, but many still can not believe that it really happened. It is an issue that will keep coming back like a boomerang. In fact, it has been an issue for the last hundred years since the Aborigines Protection Board adopted a policy in 1890 of removing mixed descent children from their families to integrate them into mainstream European society. The policy required all mixed-blood boys and girls, aged 14 and older, to leave the station to find jobs for the boys, and apprenticeships for the girls at what was called 'training homes.' More power was given to the government in the removal of children from their families. By 1921, 81% of children removed were girls and the majority were apprenticed to white homes. For a decade after this period, lighter skin Aboriginal children were placed in foster care with non-Aboriginal families. Around 300 of them were in foster homes and another hundred at the Cootamundra or Kinchela Training Institution, a boy's home. Changes in this strategy 'to help' the indigenous people have a better life continued to the late 1960s when the NSW Aborigines Welfare Board was abolished, leaving thousands of children in institutions and family homes. The story of the 'black century' became a national disgrace in 1995 when the Human Rights and Equal Opportunities Commission Inquiry into the stolen generation was tabled in Federal Parliament. It would take almost two decades again before the Australian government acknowledged this darkest part of Australian history and said sorry to the descendants of the original inhabitants of this country. The decision seemed to reflect the adage that, by acknowledging the past, we would be able to make informed decisions for the future.

The Filipinos, as colonized people, share the same experience with the Aborigines of this country. Many Filipino expatriates are unaware of a parallel experience that the 'native' Filipinos suffered at the hands of the American colonizers whose 'white burden policy' brought them to Asia and the Pacific. During the early part of the implementation of the American 'benevolent assimilation' policy, many Filipinos were displaced from their lands and separated from loved ones, relatives and families. One such story belongs to the family of Marlon Fuentes, whose great grandfather, named Markod, a Bontoc Igorot young warrior, and his family, were among the 'native' Filipinos brought to the United States to be exhibited at the St. Louis World Fair, officially known as the Louisiana Purchase Exposition of 1904. It was the largest international exposition the world had ever known. The world fair featured a wide expanse of 1,576 buildings, man made lakes, exotic flora and fauna, and big transit crowds everyday, and spread over 517 hectares of land in St. Louis, Missouri, then the fourth largest city in the United States. The Fair started on 30 April and ended on 1 December 1904, with fifty foreign countries participating, showcasing their respective cultures, products, and people. Twenty million people visited the Fair.

A Filipino reservation or village was recreated inside the 1,290 acres of land, complete with their typical habitation of the newly colonized Philippine islands. It was the most visited in the Fair, a successful money making venture for the government, at the expense of Filipinos, many of them just wearing their g-strings while being viewed by the curious public. It was also a political decision of the Americans with a 'hidden agenda': portray Filipinos as primitives, savages and barbarians and to showcase newly established reforms and educational programs initiated by the Americans in the Philippines. It was to convince the Democrats and the Anti-Imperialists that the Philippine 'insurrections' against American rule had ended and peace had been achieved. At the same time, it was to show the skeptics of the benevolent intention of America civilizing its 'little brown brothers', while negating the 300 hundred years of Catholic experience of the Filipinos. More than 50,000 exhibit items from the Philippines were displayed at the Fair, excluding in this number the human objects brought all the way from their habitat in remote places of the Philippines.

At the opening of the world fair the Filipinos joined the parade, ushered in by a *carabao*-drawn carriage and followed by thousands of people, who mesmerized the American audiences. When the marching Filipinos approached the grandstand, the loudspeaker announced and introduced: '... the Department of Anthropology prepared an assemblage of Filipinos from the Philippine islands culled from their respective villages and habitation...' The total inventory, like museum objects, was 1,130 Filipinos, composed of 38 Visayans, 78 Moros, 34 Negritos, 84 Tinguians, 25 Igorots, 4 Mangyans, 30 to 60 Bontoc-Ibanags, 38 Manobos, 5 'tree dwelling' Moros, 38 Lanao Moros, 40 Samal Moros, 300 Tagalogs, and others.

There were five villages in the Philippine reservation: the Negrito, Bagobo, Moro, Visayan, and Igorot, all clustered along the shores of a lake to simulate their typical communities in the Philippines. The Negrito Village had four cottages, complete with household implements in the Negritos' daily life. Forty-one Negritos lived in the village. They were short, dark-skinned people, belonging to the Australoid, Micronesian, and Melanesian-Papuan geographical stock. They had daily cultural presentations consisting of songs, dances, and simulations of their ancient rituals.

The Bagobo Village consisted of four houses and thirty-eight natives which opened late because they were quarantined upon arrival in St. Louis, having been stricken with smallpox earlier. The Bagobos, a pagan Malay tribe, originated from the southern coast of Mindanao. Their daily routine was giving performances with their 'stirring music and tribal dances' every half hour.

The Moro Village had fifteen native dwellings, seven for the Samals and eight for the Lanao Moros, typical of the prevailing Moro housing style, with no nails used in the construction. They had colourful flags billowing in the wind and some with the *sarimanok* design. Around hundred Moros lived in the village, regarded as the most civilized of the non-Christian Filipinos, and they came from Mindanao and nearby little islands. For their daily schedule, the Moros played the *gamelan*, and performed a frenzied dance which they called *moro-moro*. The Samal Moros occupied the seven stilt houses along the lake; there were forty of them composed of nineteen men, eleven women, five boys and five girls. The Lanao Moro Village included a tree house, perched on a tall tree and occupied by five tree-dwelling Moros.

The Visayan Village consisted of four acres and enclosed in a bamboo stockade. There were fifteen buildings composed of a native hut, a market, eight residential houses with basement work areas. About a hundred Visayans, including four children and two midgets, lived in the village. Their cultural show lasted thirty minutes, which was repeated many times each day, consisting of an orchestra, twelve singers, and sixteen dancers. For every show, the orchestra played a total of sixteen pieces and were noted for light Spanish airs and dancing music, and this continued as visitors scrutinized every portion of the ensemble, like living animals in a zoo.

In the Igorot Village consisting of a dozen houses, they were asked to build their community using materials brought all the way from the Far East. The Igorots belong to a mixture of Indonesian and Malayan strains who live in the Cordillera region of northern Luzon. They consisted of the Bontocs, Suyocs, and Tinguians, and about one hundred fourteen of them lived in the village. Like the other tribes, they were carted like cargo and animals and shipped to America for the curiosity of the 'civilized' Americans. No other exhibition was more sought after than the Filipino reservation. It was the main feature and became very popular to almost all visitors to the Fair. It was an Igorot village transported to America, complete with all the trimmings of a 'civilized' native habitation. The American idea was to make the Igorots at home, like the theme parks of today, where they slaughter and eat dogs, their 'favorite delicacy', dance their rituals, hunt, marry, give birth to countless children, and some even died, while being watched by the world fair visitors. It was a deception, because eating canine meat was not a daily fare of the Igorots. It was mainly done during rituals. The Igorot rituals in the village were sustained by the steady supply of twenty dogs a day [other sources claimed a week] by the government. The need for dogs as part of the many rituals held during the Fair resulted in the rumour that the Igorots were sneaking out of the fairgrounds at night to capture stray dogs for the next day's meal. There was also the news that local youth with business acumen rounded up dogs in their vicinity and sold them to the Igorots for as much as '$2 a piece.' As a result, the dog population of Missouri dwindled in number. In *The Official History of the St. Louis World's Fair,* an article about 'Filipinos at the Fair' written by John W. Hanson for the Louisiana Purchase

Exposition Company in 1905, described how the Igorots performed their dog feasts. 'They first bind the dog to a stick, cut its throat, while the tribesmen mumble something. It is then skinned and roasted, and eaten. The teeth of the dogs, carefully preserved, were polished, mounted and sold as souvenirs. The ritual elicited a mixture of shock and delight among the fairgoers.'

The Philippine reservation was heavily promoted by the government. In fact, two departments were created just to do marketing of the Filipino exhibits from the very beginning: the Publicity Department and the Exploitation Department, headed by two experienced newspapermen. Promotion was undertaken, both domestic and internationally. Writing about the works of the media groups, author Jose D. Fermin described the media frenzy in his book entitled *1904 World's Fair: The Filipino Experience*: 'Both departments believed they could achieve the best result not from attempting to bring people to St. Louis, which was the primary job of the Louisiana Purchase Exposition's own publicity department, but from attempting to lure people who were already in St. Louis to visit the Philippine exhibit. Therefore, the Publicity Department worked with the local press; its writers produced about 90 percent of all the Philippine articles appearing in about 400 local newspapers. The Sunday issues carried over three columns of Philippine news; hardly a weekday passed without an article about the Filipino exhibits. The articles were often accompanied with photographs, also supplied by the Publicity Department, which had a collection of about 273 glass negatives and 4,900 prints. For the smaller papers, the Publicity Department loaned them screen halftone cuts and zinc etchings to carry a general story.' We are talking only of one department here. The Department of Exploitation prepared and distributed millions of booklets and over 120,000 bird's-eye-views of the Philippine Exposition, not to mention the hundred thousands of handbills, posters and special programs to publicize the Philippine Day which was held in August of that year. There were 600 free tickets given to teachers aimed at encouraging them to bring their students to the Filipino villages. Its foreign promotion required the production of publicity materials in English, German, Spanish, French and Portuguese. There was even a request from promoters of the Fair to have General Emilio Aguinaldo, who by then was already under the control of the American authorities, brought to the Fair for people to ogle at him, as another major attraction of the exhibition. Aguinaldo was lucky that he escaped sure humiliation.

It was the American public's long awaited glimpse of the newly colonized Filipinos in the flesh. The popular human exhibits became a showcase of a new found 'primitive' population liberated by the Americans. It was an ego trip for many Americans. Marlon Fuentes claimed that their ancestors became celebrities, as in many popular reality TV shows today.

But like the rest of the Filipino exhibits of people, animals and objects, Markod never returned home. Fuentes, in retelling the story of his grandfather, believes that there is a larger story behind the disappearance of Markod and his people after the exhibition ended. Despite the carnival features of the villages, the cycle of life – births, deaths, and courtships, including weddings, which outnumbered other social activities – went on in the different villages.

As live museum objects, the Filipino natives settled into their respective quarters on the reservation; they continued with their daily lives, including the rituals practiced by the Igorots where animals, including dogs, were sacrificed for the traditional occasion. A few years later, when the exhibition was dismantled and gone, a similar sight was observed by William D. Boyce, an American journalist and publisher who had seen an Igorot village when he visited the Philippines in 1914. He attended a dog market day in Baguio where he witnessed 'About a thousand half-starved, yelling curs [are] dragged up to the mountains to be sold to the dog-eating Igorots.'

Boyce continued, 'As early as evening of Friday dogs begin to arrive in the dog section of the market and by Saturday night the section, which is purposely assigned to them by the municipal authorities, is crowded. Sunday was dog market day and early in the morning hundreds of Igorots have come down the trails to Baguio with the men clad in old coats and g-strings while their partners, the little brown women in homespun skirt and blouses, laden with baskets on their backs, held by a thong over the forehead, followed them quietly. The women, according to the foreign observer, were coming only to sell a little produce. They are not the shoppers. Dog-buying is 'man's work,' he observed. The American writer also said that the Igorots like their dogs thin. After the purchase, dogs are fattened with rice for two weeks before they are prepared for the big feast.

Like in the exhibition at the reservation where Americans curiously watched the 'native' Filipinos go about their lives, he watched how a dog was prepared: 'they take a long, sharp rattan and run it through the live dog. Then they tie the rattan to posts on both sides of the fire. They swing the dog round and round for about fifteen minutes and, when he is half cooked, they cut him up in small pieces and eat everything but the feet and tail. The tail is considered fit only for an enemy. When the meat is being served, they all sit around the fire, with their bolos upright between their toes, and tear the meat into smaller bits on the edge of the sharp knives, scorching it again before eating. It is anything but a pleasant sight.'

Of course, as with the indigenous Australians, many of the Filipino natives were forced to live a regimented life, and became the subject of countless 'scientific studies' by American scientists who found in them a rich source of laboratory specimens. Movements by Filipinos were controlled, like the Aborigines in Australia. It was similar to the concentration policy of the American military government during the Filipino-American War where 'thousands and thousands of people, mostly children, women, and old men, congregated in a very small place, without work nor means of living, many of them without a home, starving and dying from inanition, ...' Some of the human exhibits ended up in museums and laboratories long after the St. Louis Fair was finished. Fuentes viewed many of them preserved at the Smithsonian Institute. Brains in jars, skulls lining an exhibition cabinet, and hundreds of photographs of the 'native' Filipinos measured and studied. They became the subject of many articles in scientific journals that brought fame to the scientists and their institutions.

Despite his efforts, including numerous visits to museums and the Smithsonian Institute trying to track down the journey of his people, particularly his grandfather Markod, Marlon Fuentes did not find the answer to the many questions in his mind, but is still hopeful that one day his children will stumble on the destiny of their ancestors kept in musty cabinets of science laboratories and museums in America, and only then he will take a rest.

In 2004, the University of the Philippines published an extensive research undertaken by author Fermin. The author tracked down a few of the Bontoc Igorot descendants, now living in the United States: Maria 'Mia' Cristina Antero Apolinar Abeya, a descentant of Antero, and Takay, now a financial manager in the US federal government and who lives in Maryland; Antonio Buangan, a grandnephew of Pepe Betuagan and Tugamenda, now residing in San Francisco, who, like Marlon Fuentes, did considerable research to identify his descendants whom he saw in pictures at various museums and archives in the United States; and Yolanda Lacpac-Morita, a granddaughter of Buli-e Lauyan, who was in his early twenties when brought to the St. Louis as a human museum object. She is a cousin of Buangan, who migrated to the United States in 1974 and worked as a registered nurse. She lives in Tacoma, Washington. The author encountered thousands of articles published by people who were against the treatment of humans as museum objects. They were all about the degradation of Filipinos in the Philippine villages re-created for them to live in.

One interesting part of Fermin's book is the subject of an apology, the way it haunted a succession of Australian Federal governments from the time the Aborigines were recognized as inhabitants of this country and included in the official national population census. In 2000, 120 sixth-graders students of Wyndown Middle-School, which was built over the original site of the Igorot Village in St. Louis, undertook a preparation for the commemoration of the centenary of the infamous event of the 1904 World Fair where Filipinos were paraded as 'savages and barbarians' on human display. The school has established its Igorot connection through the help of Rex Botengan, officer of the Igorot Organisation in California, who assisted some of the descendants to visit St. Louis where a re-enactment of some events of the World Fair, including Igorot dances, were performed. Mia Apolinar Abeya was one of them. During the occasion, she expressed her gratitude for being invited and said '… I am deeply honored to stand here before you on the very ground that my grandfather and grandmother stood upon ninety-six years ago. We are here once more to make the gongs reverberate in their name, in the name of the Igorots, and in our children's name. For is it not the children who brought us back to this honoured place so that we may be reminded yet one more time to treat all human beings equally regardless of how we look, what we eat, how we speak, and what we wear?'

On his part, Botengan, a retired Bank of America executive, made a remark stating that times had changed and that there was no need for the students to apologize. 'I hope that they will come to know better what the Igorots are and not apologize but understand who they are and know what they are now.' Echoing a similar sentiment, the St. Louis *Post-Dispatch* said: 'Even if you can't change what happened nearly a century ago, 120 Clayton sixth-grades learned ... that the best way to make amends is to learn as much as you can about the past, and even to say you're sorry.'

At the Igorot Village where daily performances were held. Courtesy Library of Congress

The Planting of the Cross (detail) by Vicente S. Manansala. The whole of the popular painting can now be viewed at the National Gallery of the Philippines, National Museum Building. Courtesy of the National Museum

Dr. Jose Rizal, detail from a mural by Carlos 'Botong' Francisco on display at the Rizal Shrine, Fort Santiago. Courtesy of the National Historical Institute

The start of the Philippine Revolution of 1896. Photo from author's collection

Jose Rizal NHI Photo

Emilio Aguinaldo NHI Photo

An artist conception of the Philippine Independence proclamation at the Aguinaldo Mansion in Kawit, Cavite on 12 June 1898. NHI Photo

The historic Aguianaldo Mansion, now a national shrine. NHI Photo

Filipino casualties of the short-lived Filipino-American War. NHI Photo

Captured Filipino rebel leader Aguinaldo boarding the American gunboat *Vicksburg.* NHI Photo

A real Igorot village was created inside the World Fair. The Igorots were treated as human exhibits like in a reality TV show of today.   NHI Photo

The ordinary practice of the Igorots, including slaughtering of dogs for their food, was exhibited during the fair.   NHI Photo

Luna's *Spoliarium* (detail). The whole of the celebrated painting can now be viewed at the National Gallery of the Philippines, National Museum Building. From *Luna Monograph* by E. Aguilar Cruz.

Luna's *Spoliarium* was viewed at the Main Hall of the Madrid Salon during the opening in 1884 exhibition. The painter won the highest award.

The Gamboa controversy started the dismantling of the 'While Australia Policy'.
Photo taken from *Discovering Australasia*

Joyce and Lorenzo Gamboa, a symbol of successful mixed marriage between a Filipino and Australian. Photo taken a few years back when they were honoured for their contribution to the dismantling of the 'White Australia Policy'.
Bayanihan News Photo

Pura Santillan-Castrence (left) created the norm and standard, not of art, but of reality to her works that have left an imprint on the social life of Filipinos. A great lady whose legacy in literature, journalism and diplomatic history of the Philippines will always remind us how to be a true Filipino. She celebrated, in 2005, her 100th birthday with her children (below), except for a daughter and son (who were in the US and the Philippines) and grandchildren.

Bayanihan New Photos

One of the earliest foreign service offices established in Sydney, the Philippine Consulate General was first housed at the old Dunlop Building on 27-33 Wentworth Avenue, Surry Hills (above), and after the demolition of the building in 1997, a new high rise structure (left) was built on the same site through a BOT arrangement.

Bayanihan New Photos

Filipino performers were brought in from Manila for the Sydney staging of *Miss Saigon*, with Joanna Ampil (second from left) playing the title role. Bayanihan News Photo

Leo Tavarro Valdez made the role of The Engineer, a character that no one would forget, either in Sydney, Melbourne, or England performances. Bayanihan News Photo

Laurie Cadeveda took over the role of Kim in the *Miss Saigon* production in Melbourne to which she won the Helpman Award . Bayanihan News Photo

At the Sydney stage presentation of *Miss Saigon*, Joanna Ampil played the pivotal role of Kim, the Vietnamese woman. Bayanihan News Photo

Filipino Royalty?: The late President, Ferdinand E. Marcos, and his First Lady, Imelda R. Marcos. Photos from author's collection

An official reception held in Malacañang in honour of UN Secretary General Kurt Waldheim and his wife. Author's collection

The Filipino legend of *si Malakas at si Maganda* became part of the myth making associated with the Marcoses, while in power. Courtesy of the *Himalayang Pilipino*

Global Filipinos

Filipino migrants in Australia   *Bayanihan News photo*

7

Filipino migration

Recent population statistics released by the Australian Bureau of Statistics (ABS) in June 2007 show that the population of Australia is now 21 million, an increase of 315,700 people from the recorded number the same month in the previous year. NSW has the highest of the population which is 6.8M, followed by 5.2M for Victoria, 4.1M for Queensland, 2.1M for Western Australia, 1.4M for South Australia, 439,000 for Tasmania, 339,900 for ACT, and 215,000 for the Northern Territory.

Population growth figures show that the Australian population grew by 1.5% during the 12 months ending 30 June 2007. This is one of the highest population growth rates in the world. It is interesting to note that natural increase and net overseas migration contributed 44% and 56%, respectively, to the total population growth.

The ABS also revealed that all states and territories experienced positive population growth over the 12 months, with Western Australia recording the largest percentage gain (2.3%) and Tasmania the smallest (0.7%).

Based on languages spoken at home, the 2006 census revealed 15 ancestries comprising the population. The identified ancestries are Australian, English, Irish, Scottish, Italian, German, Chinese, Greek, Dutch, Indian, Lebanese, Vietnamese, Polish, New Zealander, and Filipino. This places Filipino in a significant position according to an October 2007 data of the ABS.

Blacktown in NSW has the biggest concentration of Filipino residents in Australia. In fact when the census on birth origin took place in 2006, although the dominant number of residents in Blacktown was registered at 160,480 caucasian Australians (representing 59.1% of the population), Filipinos followed with 16,128 or 5.9% of the residents of Blacktown. India followed with 2.7%, New Zealand next with 2.4%, England 2.3% and Fiji 2.0%.

Recent data made public by the Department of Immigration and Citizenship indicated that, for the period 2006-07, the total number of immigrants who arrived in Australia was 140,148, compared to 99,139 arrivals recorded ten years ago in 1996-97. Out of these current numbers, 43,835 migrants settled in NSW, 34,698 in Victoria, 28,640 in Queensland, 19,783 in WA, 10,061 in South Australia, 1,311 in ACT, 968 in Tasmania, and 843 migrants in NT. Of the total number of migrants for 2006-07, statistics show that 66,509 were males and 73,639 female.

Also we find that 19,469 migrants came from Southeast Asia, with the biggest slice coming from the Philippines, with 5,561 Filipino migrants arriving in Australia to settle down. The Vietnamese followed with 3,135 migrants; Malaysians with 2,899 migrants; Thailand with 1,989; Indonesia with 1,704; Singapore 1658; Burma 1629; Cambodia 724; Laos with 112; Brunei with 35; and East Timor with 23 migrants.

It is interesting to note that the arrival of Filipino settlers in Australia continued to grow during the last five years from 2001-02, which recorded 2,837 Filipino migrants arriving. It was followed by 3,190 arrivals in 2002-03, and for 2003-04, 4,111 Filipinos arrived. For 2004-05, there were 4,239 Filipinos who settled in Australia, and in 2005-06, 4,871 Filipinos. From the current 5,561 Filipino migrants who arrived in Australia for the period 2006-07, a total of 2,086 Filipinos decided to settle in NSW, 1,644 went to Victoria, 923 arrived in Queensland, 345 made Western Australia their final destination, 343 selected South Australia, 118 settled in Northern Territory, 53 accepted ACT, and 49 decided to live in Tasmania. Not included in these figures are other Filipinos who visited Australia during the period a short term visitors. For the period in review, 53,490 Filipinos arrived in Australia on as short term visa, a majority of them tourists. Out of this number, only 51,688 left and returned to the Philippines. What happened to the 1,802 Filipinos who were left behind? Are they now part of the growing number of TNTs (refers to Filipinos who are hiding from immigration authorities because they overstayed their visa) in our midst?

As in the previous years, many Australians departed for overseas permanently. Out of the 4,035 Australians who left the country, 356 were Filipino-Australians. This is lower compared to the 379 Filipino-Australians who decided to leave Australia for good the year before.

The unofficial figure of 200,000 Filipino migrants living in Australia will play a significant contribution to the maintenance of the Arroyo government until 2010 through their remittances of Australian dollars to their respective families back home. With the creation of additional subclass visas, including 457 work visas for skilled workers in Australia, it is expected that the number of Filipinos will increase tremendously in the years to come.

As the number of Filipino contract workers increases, tragedy and misfortune may follow them, although not in the tradition of the Middle Eastern countries where Filipinos are being beheaded or executed for the crimes they have allegedly committed, but for other situations they might be involved with. President Gloria Arroyo is not always visiting Europe and she could make a side trip to the Middle East to save or appeal clemency for her 'bagong bayani' in distress.

It should be noted that Overseas Filipino Workers (OFWs) sent back to the Philippines some US$14.6 billion in remittances, and here we are only talking of figures that actually passed through Philippine banks. What about those amounts that are hand-carried *(paki-padala)* or sent in from abroad without showing up in bank or tax records? A generous estimate is US$22 billion, the largest source of foreign income of the Philippines, exceeding by far the annual average of US$2.5 billion foreign direct investment in the country.

No wonder the government is 'pushing' Filipinos out of the country to look for the 'greener pastures', meaning more dollars, but also to disguise the fact that the incumbent and past governments cannot provide enough jobs for its people. Unemployment in the Philippines is above 8% (or about 2.8 million), and underemployment is estimated at 25% or 8.9 million of the country's workforce. If we consider the 'Population below the Poverty Line' we will have a figure of 40% of the population, which is 36.6 million, underemployed.

Wherever they go to seek for a better life, Filipinos are bound to encounter difficult lives. We have learned from the media and other sources about the fact that the life of Filipino expatriates, particularly OFWs, is often not easy. Many OFWs, both blue collar and white collar, including the undetermined TNTs, face difficult lives characterised by illegal recruitments, mysterious deaths, racial profiling, discrimination and kidnapping. In many cases, particularly in Hong Kong, China, Singapore and Middle Eastern countries like Iraq, Saudi Arabia and Lebanon, many OFWs have reported that their pay was withheld, and others who are not so lucky – their document confiscated or hidden by employers. In some cases, several sexual abuses have been committed by employers as in the case of Marilou Ranario who recently escaped death and was given life commutation by the Emir, Sheikh Sabah Al Ahmed Al Sabah upon intercession by GMA.

Recent news coverage by the *Sydney Morning Herald* highlighted the plight of Pedro Balading, who was a university-qualified piggery supervisor. He came to Australia via subclass 457 visa and assigned by his employer to general farm work in violation of the skilled visa scheme. Balading was one of the three foreign workers on 457 visas who has died in workplace incidents in 2007. There seems to be a pattern of exploitation, according to newspaper reports. Aside from Balading, another Filipino, Wilfredo Navales, and a Chinese man, Guo Jian-Dong, who were brought to Australia under 457 visas also died in workplace incidents.

In an accident currently being investigated, Balading died when he was thrown to his death from the back of speeding utility in the Northern Territory. The victim's family back in the Philippines is still lucky, in a sense, because they don't have to beg from the Overseas Workers Welfare Administration (OWWA) or the Philippine government for financial assistance. Under the workplace law being implemented in Australia, his widow, Maria Magdalena, received a life insurance lump sum in line with her entitlement, while the case of her husband's death is still being investigated by the Northern Territory Coroner's office. Mrs. Balading, as we go to press, is still awaiting news about a trust fund provision for her children, aged five, three and two. 'I have not yet recovered from the loss of my husband. I am still crying at times. I remember him in quiet moments. Time will tell when I can be healed.'

Another case is that of Wilfredo Navales, a stonemason, who arrived under a 457 visa in Western Australia for a stoneware company. Novales was the sole breadwinner for his mother, Victoria,

74, his sister Gloria, and Gloria's son Emmanuel, 8, who has Down syndrome. With 20 years experience as a stonemason in the Philippines and the Middle East, he was given unskilled jobs such as warehouse and factory work. In one such job he was asked to help in steadying two slabs of stone, three metres long by one and a half metres wide, in the upright position of an A-frame structure on which they usually rested. Contrary to work regulations, he wore no helmet, no gloves and no protective footwear. In the following incident, Navales lost balance and the slabs came over him, fatally striking his right temple.

A former workmate, Massimo Cau, who remains angry that Mr. Novales was doing unsafe work that he was not meant to be doing, said. 'I still don't understand what happened. A civilised country would find out the truth, whatever it is. This is the difference between a civilised Australia and an uncivilised Australia.' Would they have been like that if it was an Australian worker?'

There is an estimated 11 million Filipino expatriates who have suffered tremendous loneliness, isolation and dislocation. They are found throughout the world enduring 'a life of lonely, risky sacrifice.' These are the people whose remittances, estimated at around $12 billion annually or about 10% of gross domestic product, keep the Philippine economy afloat.

No wonder therefore that the government pursues a policy of encouraging Filipinos to look for jobs overseas even if they do not provide long term productivity to the nation. In fact, it is agreed by political observers that despite the seemingly vibrant Philippine economy due to these remittances, the government is increasingly becoming dependent on earnings coming from abroad to survive. But it is failing to direct these finances coming from abroad into productive investments such as education, health and job generation. A recent survey shows that most of the money sent home by Filipino expatriates is used to buy consumer goods, instead of being funnelled into productive investments.

Meanwhile, it is alarming to learn about the recent revelation made by the National Statistical Coordination Board (NSCB) stating that the income gap between the rich and poor is narrowing, and the Filipino middle class is shrinking as many of them have been joining the low-income group. This situation has happened just in a span of six years between 1997 and 2003 according to the 2006 Family Income and Expenditures Survey conducted by the NSCB.

According to Mr. Romulo Virola, NSCB board Secretary General, the shrinking of the middle class continued in 2006 and he appealed to development planners to do something for the middle class because in the end, if the situation is not abated, it will affect the prosperity of the country. Generally, it is believed that, for a country to be truly and sustainably prosperous, there must be a broad-based middle class that serves as a stabilising influence on society.

'We can no longer ignore the seemingly systematic shrinking of the group of professionals and skilled workers who can spell the difference between us being mired in poverty or crossing over to the league of First-World countries by 2020,' Virola said.

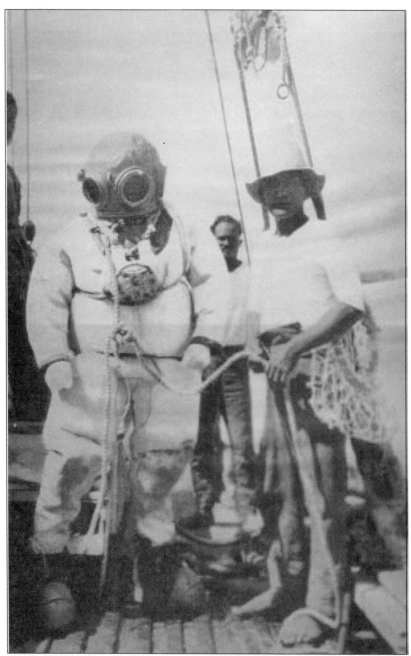

Early Filipino Overseas Workers in Australia were pearl divers
Courtesy John Oxley Library

8

First Filipino settlement in Australia

Filipinos are a globe trotting people. Eight million of them are, in fact, residing overseas, and almost in every part of the world you will find a Filipino. The first mention of a Filipino globe traveling person was during the exploration period. Enrique de Malaca, the Malay interpreter and slave of Ferdinand Magellan, was said to be a native of the Philippine islands. Enrique was taken from the East by his master to Europe, and back to the Philippines in 1521. Through his knowledge of the Visayan dialect, he became the mediator between the indigenous inhabitants of the Philippines and the explorer.

In 1619, Captain Sebastian de Pineda of Mexico City reported to King Phillip III concerning a Filipino colony in Mexico in the 17th century. The report mentioned that many Filipinos, mostly deserters from the Manila-Acapulco galleons, were living in Acapulco, Navidad, and Colima. Historical records reveal that the Filipinos were actually exiled to Acapulco in 1589 after the Tondo conspiracy. But it is a fact that the Galleon trade period also resulted in many Filipino ordinary seamen deciding to settle down in Mexico and very few ever returned to the Philippines. In 1862, a Filipino seaman of the Confederate raider, *Alabama*, which visited Cape Town, South Africa, decided to start a new life there. He became successful, and because of this more Filipinos followed. The early Filipino adventurers joined him and organised a Filipino colony. The early Filipino seamen where either 'steersmen or quartermaster' on American ships during their Pacific voyage. They established Filipino colonies in New Orleans, Philadelphia and Boston.

In the early 1870s, the difficult political and economic situation in the Philippines drove many Filipinos, some forcibly by the Spanish colonial government, outside of their birth country. Many settled in the neighboring British territories and colonies close to the Philippines. The aftermath of the Cavite Mutiny of 1872 caused many Filipinos to be exiled in Guam and the Marianas, then under the political administration of the colonial government in Manila. Many of these Filipinos eventually escaped from their detention and re-appeared in Hong Kong, Singapore, Europe, and a few in Australia. They joined the Filipinos who settled there earlier for economic reasons.

The establishment of the pearling industry in Australia in the late 1860s attracted many Asian adventurers, mostly from the 'Malay peninsula', to Northern Australia. As the Indonesians participated in the fledgling marine industry in Torres Strait, many of their brothers in the Philippines joined them and contributed their share in the rapid expansion of the industry. In fact, Australia was so attractive to Asian settlers that during the entire period of the lucrative pearling industry (1874-1940s), five major Asian communities were developed and defined the Asian diaspora in Northern Australia, particularly in the Torres Strait. A Filipino diaspora was considered one of the important pillars of the Asian diaspora that included the Chinese, Indonesians, Japanese, and Sri Lankans. The different Asian diaspora were characterized by 'a history of dispersal, myths/ memories of the homeland, alienation in the host... country, desire for eventual return, ongoing support of the homeland, and a collective identity importantly defined by this relations.'

The first recorded arrival of Filipinos was as early as 1874 when the pearling industry was at its infant stage. But there is a possibility that as early as 1842, when the City of Sydney was incorporated, that Filipinos were already residing in the city, although this is still to be confirmed. As early as 1840, there was already an existing and permanent shipping link between Sydney and Manila. Many of the laborers, particularly divers in the pearling industry, were taken from Sydney by the early pearlshell traders. Like their Muslim brothers in the southern Philippines, the early Filipino settlers reached Australia looking for jobs, via various British territories, as in the case of the indentured laborers who came from Singapore and Hong Kong in the 1870s to work in the competitive pearl shelling industry. But the possibility of them being hired directly in Manila and brought to Thursday Island can not be discounted.

The adventurous Filipinos, like those from the Malaysian archipelago, were willing to work for lower wages compared to white divers. Moreover, the Malays, and the Filipinos, in particular, could be trained as capable divers. They were responsible, daring, and fatalistically brave and had a different approach to the dangerous task in pearl shelling operations. They were venturesome, fearless and reliable. They were careless as to what depths they descended. A depth of 30 to 35 fathoms became an ordinary dive for Filipino divers.

As a consequence of the popularity of Filipino divers, a small Filipino community emerged on Thursday Island. It was a sizeable community, given the small population of Colonial Queensland at that time. Thursday Island is located on the extreme part of north-eastern Australia. It is the smallest, but the most central and important among the Prince of Wales group of Islands.

As speculated earlier, Filipinos might have first arrived in Australia during the late 1860s. What is certain, though, is that on 21 June 1880, a Filipino named Maximo Gomez, also known as Pedro, was executed by the Queensland Prison authorities in Brisbane Gaol for the crime of murder. The *Brisbane Courier* published a sketchy report about the execution. According to the newspaper, Gomez, who was tried in Cooktown in April 1880, was found guilty of murdering William Clarke of Possession Island in the Torres Strait. The case was a result of a drinking quarrel that led to Gomez striking Clarke on the head with a piece of wood.

Another source states that, prior to the introduction of the diving dress in 1874, there were already Filipinos working in the pearling industry in the Torres Strait. In 1901, testifying to the early part of the industry, William Noetke, a pioneer in the pearl shelling industry, stated that as early as 1874 Filipinos, together with Pacific Islanders, were already engaged as divers employed by Sydney operators who exported the shells. This was less than two decades after Queensland became independent from New South Wales in 1859.

In 1885, the Government Resident on Thursday Island reported that the island Filipino population numbered 'one hundred and forty seven, higher than the number of Japanese who were also engaged in the industry.' The following year, many of the Island's big pearl shelling operators, with a large number of vessels, moved to the northwest coast where vast new shell beds were discovered. Many Filipinos joined their employers in Broome, Western Australia, which became the main headquarters of the pearling industry in Australia. Between 1879 and 1901, there were 99 known Filipinos working in the Western Australian pearling industry.

By 1890, there were only 25 Filipinos left on Thursday Island. The following year, however, the number increased to 61, all males. In the neighboring little islands that are scattered throughout the Torres Strait, the presence of Filipinos was also reported. At Horn Island alone, there were fifteen Filipino residents comprising the small Filipino community there, while on the Prince of Wales Island, seventeen were listed. There were 24 Filipinos on Goode Island and 46 were known at Waier Island, while, at the least populated Hammond Island, two Filipino residents were noted.

In research written for the book *Navigating Boundaries: The Asian Diaspora in Torres Strait*, Anne Shnukal described the self-reliant Filipino community in Ngarupai (Horn Island) as '... a small number of naturalized Filipino divers, who had married local indigenous women and had become marine entrepreneurs. Their main motivation was apparently their desire to raise their families among countrymen of like mind, away from the crowded condition of Port Kennedy, and to pursue their economic interests without constant oversight.' The Filipinos on Horn Island, indeed, were treated well by the colonial authorities. They were 'generally left alone by local authorities because of their 'long residence and good behavior'.

Many of the vessels that went to Broome returned to Thursday Island in 1889 and 1890, mainly because the depleted shell beds in the Torres Strait had recovered and more shells beds had been located. Moreover, the cyclone that devastated Broome and caused heavy loss of life and destruction of numerous boats contributed to the pearlers packing their belongings and returning to Thursday Island.

In the Australian pearling industry, Filipinos played a major role not only as crew members, divers and supervisors, but also as employers or owners of fishing fleets. The year 1899 was a significant year for the Filipinos in this industry. Out of the 334 Filipinos engaged in pearl shell, bêche-de-mere, and tortoise shell fishing in the Torres Strait during that year, fifteen were owners or operators of boats, while 36 worked as masters or 'persons in charge'. There were 54 divers and 229 members of crews.

Due to the nature of their work, it was not surprising that Filipinos living in these islands were almost entirely males. Filipinos brought very few women with them, unlike the present migration pattern which is female-dominated. It was only in 1892 that Filipino women and children started to appear in the annual population statistics for Thursday Island. Eight Filipino women and 30 children were known to be living on the island that year, bringing the total number of Filipinos residing there to 98. During this time, Filipinos on the Island were already highly regarded as the only fully-integrated Asians. They were considered good and permanent members of the community. Most of them were married and had become naturalized. By then, the Filipinos were considered the 'most skilful of all divers... and exceedingly careful.' In 1895, there were 119 Filipinos on the Island. Describing the early Filipinos, John Douglas, the Government Resident for Thursday Island between 1885 and 1897, said: 'When they [Filipinos] have made a little money, they send an order home for a wife, they then marry, beget children, and frequently become naturalized.'

Except for the case of the thirteen Filipinos, two of them women, who in 1896 were issued summonses by the Sydney City Inspector of Nuisance, Reymond Seymour, for violating City health regulations, easy integration with the community has been a significant feature of Filipino migrations to Australia, even to the present time. In fact, the current family reunion policy of the government provides a stimulus for Filipino residents in Australia to sponsor relatives from home. The growth of the Filipino communities before and now can be considered a phenomenon, as close family ties is one of the distinguishing traits that Filipinos are able to maintain while residing outside their country of origin.

The high regard accorded to the early Filipinos by the authorities was also manifested by the members of the community. James Clarke, a noted pearl sheller and owner of one of the biggest pearl shelling companies operating in the Torres Strait, told the Royal Commission investigating the pearling and bêche-de-mere industry in 1898 about the industriousness and reliability of Filipinos. Clarke testified that a Filipino diver can work 'day after day, year in and year out'. Some of them worked for him for more than twenty years.

On the other hand, the Japanese, although treated as 'desirable employees', were criticized for being ambitious, aggressive and a predilection for personal advantage – in general, a Japanese's ambition was initially to become a diver then finally a boat owner, thereby posing a threat to both the caucasian ship owners and other 'colored' labor. Testifying at the 1897 Commission on Pearl Shell and Bêche-de-Mere Fisheries, Percival Pitman Outridge, managing partner of James Clarke and Company, said that the common feeling was very strong against the Japanese and that the 'colored' men had forgotten their little differences and clubbed together against the Japanese. According to Outridge, the Japanese had driven the caucasian divers out of the industry, along with other nationalities like the Filipinos. During this period, Thursday Island was already known for its multi-cultural community. No less than 25 nationalities were reported residing on the Island.

The life of the Filipinos in the pearling industry was not only reflected in the different accounts of the ruthless competition posed by the Japanese, who eventually displaced them from their high place in the industry, but also on racial issues affecting Asians, or 'colored' men, as they were regarded then. As Asians, the early Filipinos in Australia seemed not directly affected by the 'White Australia Policy'. Because of the distance between Thursday Island and the more populated areas of Brisbane, Sydney or Melbourne, inhabited mostly by migrants from Anglo-Celtic backgrounds, the impact of the policy on Filipinos was not as strong as it was on the Chinese and Japanese.

In some lighter moments, the Filipinos had been the subject of several published works which romanticized and vividly captured the Filipino spirit and their longing for their country of origin. In *Forty Fathoms Deep – Pearl Divers and Sea Rovers in Australian Seas*, the author described Castilla Toledo, a Filipino diver and the main character of the novels, as :

> '... a handsome Manillaman [Filipino], a flash diver... Tall and lithely built, his youthful, light brown skin allied to speaking brown eyes, coal-black hair and flashing teeth made him almost an Adonis. He was strong too, his well-knit frame active with a cat-like grace. At sea, dressed only in a *sarong*, he was sulky or savage or merry just as his mercurial temper dictated. But at Broome, with his bright shore smile, and smartly dressed in the flash Manila way, he was laughing, hail-fellow-well-met, pleasant company. In the starlit evenings on the foreshore he would strum the guitar while his soft, melodious voice was plaintively expressive in the love-songs of old Manila.
> ... From the *Phyllis* came the twang of guitar, then Toledo's silvery voice. Around him dusky Manillamen [Filipinos], dreaming with the song, centuries of racial antipathy separating them from the Malay.'

The Filipino community did not come out unsullied during the difficult years of the industry in the mid-1890s. Aside from racial tension they had to contend with, caucasian fleet owners constantly jolted the industry by their vigorous campaign on Thursday Island and in Brisbane for discriminatory legislation preventing Asians from participating in the entrepreneurial side of the pearl shelling industry. As a matter of fact, a government prohibition was already being implemented in Broome and Darwin.

Moreover, natural and man-made causes brought problems to the otherwise peaceful Filipino community of Thursday Island. Due to competition for better harvests, divers were forced to dive in deep waters. There was a strong eagerness to make a good score characterized by strong reckless rivalry between competing divers. Precautionary measures for diving in deep water were disregarded or completely ignored. A great number of divers became paralyzed. This practice resulted in the untimely deaths of healthy, able-bodied and experienced divers. In 1892, the peaceful community of Thursday Island was shocked by the deaths of five caucasian divers. Out of the 24 reported deaths for that year, nine were Filipinos. Every year thereafter, Filipinos divers became part of the annual returns submitted by the Government Resident on Thursday Island. One Filipino diver died in 1894; two in 1895; and four in 1896.

In another incident, six Filipinos were murdered by Aborigines in 1893. The first case took place on the west coast of the Cape York Peninsula and involved the killing, by two Batavia River boys, of two Filipinos, named Pascal and Kintur, owners of the cutter *Leonore*. The police reported that the murder case resulted from an allegation that the Filipinos took the gins [wives] of the Aborigines away from them. The other case happened off Boyden Cay on the east coast. The incident arose from the shipping of seven Aborigines from the Pine River area to work in the pearling industry. It is not known whether the Filipinos were guilty of 'black birding', kidnapping Aborigines (an illegal activity) for cheap labor in the industry, a common practice during those days. Four Filipinos died instantly, while the last, who was seriously wounded in the head by a tomahawk, died in hospital. The murderers were never caught and the case became part of the long list of unsolved crimes in colonial North Queensland.

That the members of the Filipino community were peace loving is proven by the good regard accorded them as permanent components of the pearl shelling industry. As a group, they were known for their kinship orientation and strong Filipino traits. One of these common traits was loyalty to a friend or to a benefactor. Do a Filipino a little favor and he would remember it to the end of his days. The late historian Professor Teodoro Agoncillo said:

> '... to the Filipino, friendship is sacred and implies mutual help under any circumstances. A friend is expected to come to the aid not only of a personal friend, but also for the latter's family. A man's friend is considered a member of the family and is expected to share its tribulations as well as its prosperity and happiness. It is almost unthinkable for the Filipino to betray his friend, and if there be such one, he becomes a marked man: ostracism is the lightest punishment that can be meted out to him.'

Notwithstanding the 'White Australia Policy', the Filipino presence in North Queensland continued. In fact, between 1901 and 1910 there was a steady arrival of Filipinos exempted from the provisions, particularly the dreaded dictation test, of the Immigration Restriction Act 1901-1910. There were 98 Filipinos admitted to Australia in 1902. Ninety-five Filipinos were destined for the pearling industry, while two were returning residents and one came from within the Commonwealth to work as a servant. Out of 22 Asians admitted to the Northern Territory during the first two months of 1901, three were Filipinos, while in Western Australia 105 males and one female were allowed entry to the colony during the same year. In 1904, 54 Filipinos were allowed to enter Australia. Forty-four of them were recruited for the pearling industry, while nine were returning residents and one was on a temporary entry permit. Eighteen Filipinos were allowed entry in 1907 and the same number in 1908. In 1910, sixty six Filipinos were granted temporary entry permits and sixteen of them to work in the pearling industry, while one was a returning resident. Fifty of the group came direct from the Philippines and 16 arrived from the 'Straits Settlements.'

The continual arrival of Filipinos in Australia contributed to the racial attitude of white Australians towards Asians. Although praised for their docility and other positive traits, except for some cases of unexplained outburst, the Filipinos created a negative reaction from white Australians because they belonged to what was then commonly considered a dreaded detestable race – the Asiatics or 'colored men.'

Commenting on the expected arrival of an additional 150 Filipinos on Thursday Island in 1899, the *Newcastle Morning Herald and Miners' Advocate* apprehensively commented:

> 'At the present time there are many reasons why Filipinos should not be encouraged to come in large numbers to this country. Apart from the general objection to fill [sic] this land with hordes of Asiatic aliens, it cannot be forgotten that Filipinos have recently made themselves notorious by coming into rough contact with white men.'

The number of Filipinos living in Australia was reduced when the supply of pearl shells was depleted. Many of them, particularly those without families, returned to the Philippines and engaged in new ventures. Although the new sources of pearl shells were discovered in Broome, Western Australia, the size of the Filipino communities never recovered. The last blow was the effect of the White Australia Policy which finally caught up with them. The official census of 1904 listed 188 Filipinos engaged in the marine industry on Thursday Island. This number was reduced to 52 Filipinos during the following year and the number continued to decrease. According to official records of the government and no Filipinos appeared in the census until 1911 when 444 Filipinos were listed as residing in NSW, Victoria, Queensland, West

Australia and Northern Territory. They again re-appeared in 1921 with 329 Filipinos. They started to re-appear in the census in 1930 until 1938 but very small number remained in the industry.

Today, what remains on Thursday Island, particularly on Horn Island, are the descendants of the pioneer Filipino settlers who had intermarried with the indigenous inhabitants of the place. Their village where they live has been described as typical of the 'second-generation Asian-Indigenous communities of Torres Strait.' The second-generation families, according to a study, were united by 'kinship and affinal' relationship rather than of their country of origin.'

In *Navigating Boundaries: The Asian Diaspora in Torres Strait*, Monica Walton Gould, one of the remaining links that connect with the surviving Filipino diaspora in Torres Strait, tells of her family story. She was born to William Walton and Gregoria (Guria) Assacruz in 1927. She is identified as a Torres Strait Islander and of Aboriginal, Filipino and English heritage extraction. She married Harold Andrew Gould after the war and produced eight children and 17 grandchildren.

Recalling her younger life on Torres Strait, she said: 'I was born on Thursday Island. I don't know if it was in hospital or at home, probably at home. We lived in John Street, not in Malaytown. Malaytown was up the other end past the Post Office. John Street was nearer the shopping centre in Douglas Street, in the middle. We didn't go down to Malaytown. In our days, Catholics mixed only with Catholics. I don't know why. There was something about religion in those days.

> '... Mum was always busy, cooking dampers, cooking the fish, cooking the rice. I didn't know her parents, they weren't alive by then. Mum never spoke about her family. Dad was a very strict man and he had the little sailing boat, *Valmay*. Dad used to go across to Thursday Island every day to work...

'... Dad sometimes used to make *tuba*; he was no innocent. I remember seeing him take a hanging bunch of coconut blossoms, tying them all together and bending them over an earthenware pot. The juice dripped into the pot and when it was fermented enough, they drank it. Dad used to be very happy some evenings. Mum asked him to keep some of it for her to ferment more to make vinegar. She used to make a coconut oil to wash our hair. You let it boil and boil and it turns into coconut oil. You can cook with it, use it on the skin to counteract the heat, and use it for washing your hair.'

The bond that developed between the Torres Strait Indigenous and various Asian communities, including the Filipinos, resulted in cultural cross pollination which, according to the same study cited above and can be gleaned in contemporary Torres Strait 'religion, food, cooking practices, plants, gardening techniques, clothing, architecture, household implements and cooking utensils, mortuary rites, music and dance, as well as vocabulary borrowed into the Torres Strait languages from Malay, Japanese, Tagalog and Chinese...'

Also, the study pointed out that other aspects of Asian interaction with Torres Strait Indigenous people endured and became 'nativised'. Some of these aspects 'were integrated into pan-Islander custom, changed to some degree to conform to existing local custom and generally recognized as part of contemporary *ailan pasin* (island custom). It was confirmed that the incorporation of cultural borrowing into contemporary *ailan pasin* was easily achieved through 'nativisation' and widespread distribution. Various cultural borrowings were grouped into four cultural domains, namely: food (ingredients, condiments, recipes, preparation and cooking methods, utensils); mortuary rites; the lexicon of local languages; and music and dance.

Thursday Island in the early 1900s. From *The Sydney Mail*, 1899.

9

Are Filipino associations relevant?

Picture a mother and her fourteen-year old son languishing in Villawood Immigration Detention Centre, a place described by a Rooty Hill High School student and a friend of the boy, as 'like a real prison with razor wire and guards.' Add to this scenario the much publicized wrong detention and deportation of Australian citizen, Vivian Alvarez.

The mother and son are still inside the Villawood detention centre, while Vivian Alvarez-Solon, who recently created news when she was discovered living in a hospice in Olongapo City four years after she was wrongfully removed from Australia because 'no one would take care of her' Down Under, negotiated with the Australian government for her return to Australia.

Faced with the above scenario, many concerned Filipino residents might wonder what became of the 22 Filipino TNTs caught near Griffith in NSW a couple of years ago. The Filipino TNTs were found working in breach of their tourist visas. They were also detained at one of the notorious detention centers, mostly at the Villawood Immigration Detention Centre, maintained by the Australian government. Their tourist visas were subsequently cancelled.

The highest number of detainees is held at the Villawood Detention Centre. The total number of residents detained at these detention centres, according to statistics released by the

Department of Immigration and Multicultural and Indigenous Affairs, is 6,196 persons, as of 25 June 2004. Although the majority of the detained people are Afghan, Iraqi, Iranian, Chinese, Indonesian, Sri Lankan, Palestinian, Korean, Vietnamese and Bangladeshi, there is no doubt that Filipinos are among those languishing at any of the immigration detention centers. This is evidenced by the apprehension of 22 Filipino TNTS cited earlier. What happened to them? Were they secretly flown to Manila on a plane paid for by the Australian government?

Other proof that more Filipinos might end up at any of the government detention centers is the fact that the number of Filipinos arriving in Australia on tourist visas or temporary visas is increasing. For the year 2000-01 alone, the total number of Filipinos who entered Australia on temporary visas was 43,332, comprising 1,862 temporary resident visas, 1,373 student visas, 33,016 visitor visas, and 7,081 other visas. This number jumped to 48,300 in 2002-03. In contrast, there were only 3,036 Filipinos who settled in Australia permanently, either on family or skill migration schemes.

A few years back I wrote in my book, *Brown Americans of Asia*, about the plight of Filipino 'mail order brides' and the trauma they suffered; some of them were killed by their own husbands while surviving Down Under devoid of help or assistance from any Filipino organization in the country. Given all these problems, why is it that no Filipino association has come to the rescue of these hapless persons. Are Filipino associations in Australia relevant? This was asked by a friend who has no affiliation with any of the many Filipino associations listed in souvenir programs and Filipino community newspapers. Or have they reached their end 'use-by-date' and therefore deserve to be discarded.

The main reason for organizing an association is to help its members. The same could be said for Filipino associations. They are organised, not only to help Filipino migrants settle down in Australia, but also to help them cope with the problems associated with starting a living in an entirely different community.

The ten-year old statistics obtained from the Department of Foreign Affairs show that there are no less than 216 Filipino associations in Australia, organized and aimed at helping member Filipino migrants.And that figure was taken a decade ago when the number of Filipinos in Australia had not reached hundreds of thousands. I could imagine the number of Filipino associations now, since the number of Filipino migrants in Australia has increased dramatically.

The latest figures from the Philippine Department of Foreign Affairs show that the number of Filipino associations, including one man or one-woman associations, now existing in Australia exceeded the 200 mark. Why is it then that no words were heard from these associations when our compatriots were found in a situation that required help and assistance? Are Filipino groups organized mainly to celebrate Philippine independence day or became sponsors of local shows with imported artists from Manila? Or they are operating to provide the much hyped Filipino fiesta where many organizations are actively involved. The last 2004 Fiesta Cultura event alone had more than fifty organizations listed which contributed to the success of the annual event of beauty contest, singing, food festival and others.

It seems Filipino associations are missing the very reason for their existence – to promote the welfare of Filipino migrants in Australia. Or do they exist only for the next ballroom dancing, *Pamasko* event, or Fiesta extravaganza or Fiesta Cultura? Where were they when cases such as in case of the mother and son held in the Villawood detention centre? Where were they when Alvarez was detained and wrongly deported?

One may argue that there was a group of Filipinos who tried to help in the case of Alvarez, and some Filipinos trying to make representation for the detained mother and son, but where are the Filipino groups which are expected to visibly provide assistance to Filipino compatriots in distress and trouble? My early encounter with Filipino associations in Australia took place in 1975 when I arrived in Australia for a nine-month scholarship tour Down Under. The trip took me to Brisbane, Canberra, Melbourne, Adelaide, Perth and Fremantle. During this sojourn, I had the chance to talk to the few organized groups in Australia and learned from them how they helped the new arrivals in Australia.

Are Filipino associations created merely to serve the interest of its founder, or was it to work for the interest and benefits of its members? This is not to say that the yearly Fiesta Cultura and Fiesta Extravaganza are not important. What is needed in Australia are Filipino associations that are vigilant in providing assistance or help to any Filipino member of the community who is in trouble or in distress. The problem with the current crop of Filipino associations is that they are more social clubs and they are not particularly concerned with the needs of their members. One of the big problems facing Filipino migrants in Australia is the recognition of their skills and academic qualifications obtained overseas. Why is it that no groups or association ever volunteered to work for the amendment to the *Country Profile* issued by the migration department many years ago, to enable many of their countrymen/women who are qualified to migrate to Australia. Or are there any social groups going out there in the community helping new arrivals and showing how to adjust easily in the community? Why is it that there is no association to provide help to Filipino students who are homesick or to provide English or Filipino language courses to help migrants obtain language skills that will help them achieve their easy integration into the community? Why is it that we have more associations sponsoring discos, fiestas, etc?

Filipinos vs. Pacific Islanders

It has been observed that when Filipinos are overseas they behave properly and are noted for being law abiding residents in their host countries. Rarely, one could find trouble caused by them that is reported in the media.

In Australia, as the number of Filipino migrants unofficially is reaching the 220,000 mark, we have not seen or read in newspaper accounts about the involvement of Filipinos in illegal schemes or implicated in dreadful cases that would shame the Filipino community. Except for a case reported in the papers where a young son was accused of killing his family, no other horrendous case has been reported that would merit concern within the community. The case of Sef Gonzales, the law student accused of murdering his family, has been followed by Filipino expatriates living in Australia, with the latest development stating that his bail application was rejected in the Supreme Court amidst allegations that he faked his abduction, faked his parents' death certificates and could possibly fake his own death.

Three other cases that have Filipino connections were reported in the papers most recently. One refers to Craig Andrew Merritt, 30, who admitted killing his three children by his estranged Filipina wife; the second case is about Thomas Andrew Keir who was acquitted of killing his second Filipina wife, Rosalina Canonisado, 22 years old, but jailed for the murder of his first wife, Jean; and the last case is Commonwealth Bank employee

Janilyn Serrano who was reported in the *Sunday Telegraph* to have been placed on a three year, $1000 good behavior bond, and to pay back the $37,000 she stole from the bank. Aside from the above cases, we have not heard or read in the papers about Filipino migrants, particularly those involving other ethnic groups. Although, some reports clearly described some horrendous cases involving persons of 'Asian' appearance, this writer has not found any involvement of Filipino migrants.

Relationships between Filipino migrants and other ethnic groups seems to work peacefully and there seems to exist a harmonious dealing among them, all coming to this country to seek a better life and achieve their ambition in life. Looking back, more than a century ago, the small Filipino community in Australia, primarily those living in Thursday Island, were shocked by the bloody encounter between Filipino migrants and the South Sea Islanders near the corner of Victoria Parade and Normanby Street, an offshoot of stabbing incidents in which the Pacific Islanders were accusing the Filipinos of being the aggressors. The accusation resulted in a serious rift between the two groups, whose world had been the pearling industry. The enmity disturbed the harmony existing in the multi-racial community of the Torres Strait region.

In his book, *Thirty Years in Tropical Australia,* Rev. Gilbert White, DD, who served the Diocese of Carpentaria for thirty years, first as a priest, and later as Bishop, witnessed the night confrontation or racial brawl between the 'extraordinarily law-abiding' Manilamen (the name given to early Filipinos in Australia) and the South Sea Islanders on 16 January 1900. According to Bishop White, the encounter was the culmination of a long-standing grudge between the two parties. In that incident, several Pacific Islanders were stabbed and Filipino migrants were reported as the aggressors.

In Bishop White's own account: 'The South Sea Islanders who are true sportsmen, immediately notified their opponents, and turned up the following afternoon to the number of about a hundred fighting men, armed with nothing but their fists. About sixty Manila men appeared, all armed with formidable knives. The South Sea Islanders were not daunted, and attacking with their fists soon put their opponents to headlong flight.

'I heard the battle cries from my house a few hundred yards away, and coming out on the veranda was astonished to see a man covered with blood from head to foot walking in the direction of the hospital: his companions were relieving their feelings by smashing the windows of a Manila tradesman whom they accused, probably without reason, of supplying the knives.

'The police happened to be engaged at the other end of the town, and when they arrived all was over. One South Sea Island man was killed and several badly wounded, but the Islanders were satisfied that they had gained a glorious triumph, and were proportionately grateful in their hearts to the quite conscious magistrate.'

The Manila trader reported above was Heriverto Zarcal, the most successful Filipino migrant in Queensland. He was engaged in the pearling industry, not as a diver like most of the Filipinos at that time, but as an entrepreneur. He owned a lot of properties on Thursday Island and operated more than a dozen luggers in his fleet. His business interests expanded not only in Brisbane, but also Melbourne and Sydney. In fact, he was appointed by President Emilio Aguinaldo as his ambassador to Australia during the short lived first Philippine government.

The 19 January 1900 issue of *Torres Strait Pilot*, the island's only newspaper, reported the bloody encounter. It reported: 'Some few days ago a South Sea boy only assaulted a Manilaman, inflicting several nasty wounds. This was the beginning.

The details of the development of the trouble are now ascertainable; but on Monday there were rumors of a conflict being arranged between representatives of the two peoples. This became more pronounced on Tuesday; and while the two classes seemed in no way to communicate with each other, it worked out that Wednesday evening was to see the tussle wherein the Manilamen were to avenge the assault mentioned above.'

The Manilamen tried to publicize their side in *Torres Strait Pilot* concerning their differences with the South Sea Islanders, but the newspaper refused. The newspaper account continued and said: 'Almost immediately after this a great crowd of the South Sea Islanders had assembled on the Parade, at Normanby Street, where also the Manilamen congregated. Several citizens who saw what was brewing endeavored to the utmost to frustrate the trouble. But all to no avail. A general movement of the Manilamen took place towards the Kanakas. Of the latter there must have been at least a hundred, the Manilamen probably being about half that number. Some palaver took place, the Kanakas asking to take their opponents one at a time. But these negotiations were stopped by a big South Sea boy armed with a big baton rushing on the opponents.

'He was closely followed, and stones from 2lb up to 10 lb were flying about immediately, to the consternation of the business people in the vicinity, who mostly had then put up their shutters. Some of the men got to close quarters, and as a result, where knives were used, the injuries inflicted were of a serious nature. But this did not last long. The Manilamen were outnumbered, and gave way. Some of them sought – or it was thought so – shelter at Mr. [Heriverto] Zarcal's.

'The South Sea lads, whose spirits were rising higher, then moved a fierce attack on Mr. Zarcal's shop, bombarding it with lumps of rock and in less than a couple of minutes wrecking the whole of the handsome windows and doing great damage to the stock inside. Afterwards, Mr. Zarcal's shop inside was seen to be strewn with broken glass, jewellery, clocks, and others and he sustains considerable loss. Even the iron balcony rail on the second storey of the building had been smashed through in places by the heavy stones thrown. The disorderly scene lasted only a few seconds longer. Two of the police came along, and the Kanakas, having no further desire apparently than to defeat the Manilamen, began to disperse.'

After the fracas, several men injured at the beginning were attended to. Tom Malayta, a South Sea Islander, had received a wound from a knife which had entered just the junction of the his right arm and shoulder which had penetrated deeply and severed the main blood vessels, entered the lung, and so great had been the forces of the blow and so sharp the knife that the second rib bone was half cut. He died from the wound an hour and a half later. Six other men were brought to the hospital and one treated as out-patient. Three of the seriously affected, one had his skull fractured, the operation trephining performed on him; another had a stab wound on the side, the lung penetrated; and the third received a wound just above the collarbone, perilously near the main blood vessels.

The encounter took less than five minutes. There were only three policemen in the vicinity, who were powerless to stop the fight and before others could be brought along to assist, the fighting had ceased. A meeting was held with the magistrates of the island and arranged to bring in more constables and to call the military in readiness. Hotels were ordered to be closed at six o'clock in the evening. The police and the military patrolled the town during the night, and never before was there a quieter night on the island.

'Every effort has been made to get the men to sea and at work, and probably there will be no further danger of the men fighting among themselves, notwithstanding the rumors that are flying about alliances between different classes to wipe out the Manilamen and so on,' the newspaper reported.

Of tiaras, sashes and medals

A couple of photos landed on my desk at the *Bayanihan News*. The photos were taken during the last Philippine Independence Ball. Organizers of the event stated that the photos were taken during the traditional *rigodon de honor*, a misunderstood Filipino tradition we inherited from Spain and brought to Australia.

What caught my attention were the shoulder sashes over Barong Filipino worn by men and the glittering tiaras on the well coiffured heads of the ladies in white ternos. Are the organizers of this year's independence ball starting a trend? The observance of a national day of the country is a serious affair that should be handled with dignity and respect. This is why dignitaries normally graced the occasion. I understand the then opposition leader John 'Pogi' Brogden and Labor Minister Laurie Ferguson attended the affair. Were the organizers trying to inject color and glitter into the occasion, or was it purely theatrical? Well, people who know about Filipino tradition would admit that adding tiaras and sashes was not only against protocol, but also cheapened the affair and relegated it to a community beauty pageant. To some observers, it was a costume or fancy ball attended by over excited participants. One was even sure that it was not the true traditional *rigodon de honor* being peddled around during the evening. Would the over abundance of tiaras and sashes compensate for the absence of regal and grace in execution of the steps for the *rigodon de honor*? Or did the additional fashion contraption really improve the dancing skills of the wearer? The traditional *rigodon de honor* cannot be executed gracefully by wearing tiaras and sashes. Indeed, it was all about tiaras and sashes that dominated the evening. There are many kinds of tiaras that can decorate and enhance the external look of the wearer. Some original tiaras are made of pearl, rhinestone and pearl, and crystal. And for those who are not very particular about the kind of tiaras they place on their heads, there are replicas like the Audrey Hepburn tiara, the Princess Diana tiara, or the Miss Universe crown will equally serve the purpose. Other ordinary tiaras are called flower girl tiaras, pageant tiaras, *quinceañera* tiaras, birthday tiaras, the so-called '2005' tiaras, bride-to-be tiaras, and rodeo queen tiaras. But the worst kind of tiaras are those imitation tiaras or pieces made from *puwit ng baso* (base of drinking glasses) or the plastic ones that provide good glitters and reflection from the light which are very popular among participants in local Filipino beauty contests.

History tells us that using tiaras, also known as diadems, signify nobility or royalty (Please take note participants). It is an extremely ancient custom. The first mention of the tiara was in the eighth century during the reign of Emperor Constantine when he gifted Pope Constantine a headdress. It was used for pontifical liturgical functions. It was a white headdress called phrygium. This headdress was later adorned with a royal circlet of diadem. The coins issued during the tenth century (Sergius III – 904-911) and Benedict VII 974-983) are considered the earliest illustration of the royal circlet. Eventually by the eleventh century, the word tiara referred to a circlet on the papal head-covering which appeared during the reign of Pascal II (1099-1118). The tiaras of the Eastern Kings during the ancient times were considered extremely ornate and heavy. The early Egyptians wore richer head-dresses and some of those placed on the head of Egyptian princesses were amazingly delicate. For instance, one piece belonging to Princess Khnemt is made of 'delicate flowers in gold wire, inlaid with stones, and has all the fragility of a wreath made of real wild flowers.' Another tiara made by Giuliano about 1890 was set with four large topazes. Among the Greeks are found the earliest diadems, which were made of gold or silver sheet decorated with simple patterns of dots embossed from the back. In classical times, the diadem of sheet gold decorated with embossed patterns was joined by the wreath. Extremely naturalistic imitations of wreaths of real leaves were made in gold, silver, and materials painted with gold, and were worn on ceremonial occasions.

The reason why women wear tiaras, according to tiara expert Dion Palady, is that the head ornament signifies 'hope, magic, glamour, wealth and sophistication than most woman experience in a lifetime'. There is now a tradition of passing on your own tiara to the next generation. But she is talking of real expensive tiaras. According to Palady, the tiara is better with a hair style or wedding dress. There are three ways of wearing a tiara: 1) put your hair up, wear the veil right behind the tiara, with the veil attached with a comb; 2) bun-wrap person is a good style. Put the tiara on the front of the bun, and the veil in the back, attached either with a comb or hair pins; 3) without a veil – usable on any occasion, prom, Christmas party, or any special event.

Shoulder sashes over Barong Pilipino look unusual. The only time I remember where a sash was worn over the national costume was during the time of Ferdinand Marcos whose wife, then First Lady Imelda Marcos, had a grandiose dream for the Marcos family as the first real Filipino royal family. She commissioned official portraits of Marcos standing wearing his trademark Barong Pilipino with a red, white and blue sash. Mrs. Marcos' portrait was also decorated with a sash. The same as with the family portrait. Placed over this sash is a medallion which looks like an Order of Sikatuna and on his left breast the numerous war medals he claimed to have received during his war exploits. Later, an historian exposed these medals as fakes. The look of Marcos is amusing because with the heavy medals pinned on his left breast, his *jusi barong* was not even affected by their weight. It stayed fresh, crisp and flat on his breast. As indicated below, the shoulder sash is best used over European suits, not on a flimsy Barong Pilipino. Wearing sash, either a waistband or a shoulder sash is common in Europe, and in South or Latin America. The sash is a band or ribbon worn about the waist as part of one's clothing or over the shoulder as a symbol of rank. It is only worn by presidents. Almost every nation has some form of decorative sash, mainly associated with the highest military awards. As a decorative sash, it is worn over the shoulder to the hip rather than around the waist. This tradition dates back to the 17th century in South and Latin America. Today, out of the 21 presidents of the Americas, 19 wear their presidential sashes featuring the national colors and symbols of each country. It is also a symbol of the continuity of the government. When the incumbent president completes his tenure of office or resigns, the same sash is passed on to his successor or to the new President as part of the inauguration ceremony. The United States of America and Cuba do not have presidential sashes. Another kind of sash is a cloth belt designed to hold a robe together. It is usually tied about the waist. The Japanese equivalent of a sash is used to hold a kimono or yukata together and it is called *obi*. Traditionally, sashes are part of formal military attire, and some decorations such as the *Legion d'honneur* are worn with a special sash.

We can not discuss presidential sashes without discussing medals of foreign honor such as decorations or medals. By observation quite a number of Filipino migrants are proud to wear their medals, from whatever sources they obtained them. For them I would like to state that in Australia the 'acceptance and wearing of a foreign honor such as honor, decoration or medal other than one granted by Her Majesty the Queen of Australia', is not allowed without permission from the governor-general. Some Filipinos who have a fetish about wearing medals disregard this protocol. Wearing of medals as a proof of distinguished career became a trend during the Marcos regime. The official photographs of President Ferdinand E. Marcos, First Lady Imelda Romualdez Marcos and the members of the First Family featured wearing sashes and medals. It was the height of pretentiousness in Philippine history.

At the last count, there are only about 50 official or sanctioned orders, decorations and medals in the Philippines. Excluding from these number are medals awarded by private organizations and other bodies such as the Knights of Rizal. Some of the decorations granted by the Philippine government are as follows: Congressional Quezon Service Cross, Medal of Valour, Philippine Constabulary Medal of Valour, Order of Sikatuna, Distinguished Conduct Star, Distinguished Service Star, Legion of Honour, Golden Heart Presidential Award, National Artist Award, Gawad sa Kaunlaran Medal, Order of Grieving Heart, Order of Gabriela Silang, and others.

Rigodon de Honor

One distinguishing feature of a multicultural society such as the Philippines is its dances. There is a dazzling diversity of dances from the peoples of the country, from those living in Batanes in the north down to the inhabitants of Sulu in the south. The number and type of dances of the Filipinos range from the dances of the mountain tribes of the Cordillera that recall the sculptural heights and the brave birds of the air, to the people who live by the sea. The dances of the lowland can be distinguished from the dances of the highlands. The diversity of dances relates to the geographic, climatic and cultural features of various parts of the country. No less than 40 ethno-linguistic groups or tribes comprise the population of the Philippines and many of them have unique dances that have been handed down generation to generation. Like the other facets of Filipino life, dances have various influences including Indian, Chinese, Indo-Chinese, Indonesian, Malay, Spanish and American.

Rigodon de Honor came as a product of the more than three hundred years of Spanish subjugation of the Filipinos. It emanated from European dance performed at social functions in France and known as *quadrille*. It was introduced in the Philippines as *rigodon de honor* and became known during the American period as *birginia*. It is a dance that highlighted balls in ordinary towns and cities as well as in high places, particularly the annual *rigodon de honor* held at Malacañang Palace. During the Spanish period, *rigodon de honor*, aside from being a main feature of fiesta celebrations, was performed during thanksgiving ceremonies for the successful trips of the Galleons across the Pacific. It was also performed to welcome a new governor-general or a bishop. According to cultural historian Felice Sta. Maria, 'no fiesta is complete even today without a proper *rigodon de honor* performed by the dignitaries of the town and their special guests.' Sta Maria continues to describe how the dance is performed: 'The *rigodon de honor* opens a dance. It began during the baroque age (1600-1750) in the magnificent French court. To its 4/4 beat dancers executed six basic steps: salute, zigzag, sway, visit, small and big chain. The choreography was a glamorous square dance which residents in Porac, Pampanga turned into an imaginative marvel: rigodon on horseback in the 1800s.' During the American period, often in the Manila Hotel, no ball began without a *rigodon de honor*.

In the book *Halupi: Essays on Philippine Culture*, author Sta. Maria described how the Filipinos developed a liking for a similar dance: 'Filipinos also took a fancy to waltzing. The ¾ beat became one of the most beautiful Austrian contributions to celebration in the 1800s. It was more elegant than the polka which evolved at about the same time in Europe. But the waltz, whether done moderately or quick-paced, was always elegant. Manilans danced to Kaualich's *Sur la montage, Le train de plaisir*, Fahrback's *Lagrimas* and Hoilgrano's *Carnaval*. As the days progressed, Filipino folk outside urban domain, converted the ¾ beat and turned it into various native steps executed by performers delicately during the days ladies moved about in the Maria Clara dress. When *Bayanihan Philippines* first showed the world Filipino folk dances in the 1950s, audiences were amazed at the grace, dexterity, charm and happiness of island music. From the seriousness of mountain and Mindanao ritual dances, Philippine communities created the cheerfulness characteristic of *tinikling*, jota, fandango, valse, mazurka and *rigodon de honor*.

During the 19th century, saving one's face was very important even during attending a social event such as a dance like *rigodon de honor*. To prevent men from being embarrassed when refused by the ladies whom they asked for a dance, a system of saving face in such a situation was copied from Europe and adopted in the Philippines. This was called *carnet du bal*. 'At every dance, ladies carried a *carnet du bal*, sometimes hanging from their left wrist, other times from a gold chain that was clipped onto the waistline. The carnet was a tiny notebook with its miniature pencil hidden behind covers of silver, mother of pearl, gold, ivory, tortoise shell or decorative paper boards.' The *carnet* contained a list of dances at an occasion and to whom a lady had promised each dance. It is presumed that a prior arrangement had been made between the lady and the gentlemen before the scheduled dance. With the *carnet*, gentlemen are never embarrassed by a public refusal and a woman was given the privilege to select her favorite partners. As in the past, Filipinos of Sydney are aware of the tradition reflected in the *rigodon de honor*. They perform the dance as a form of thanksgiving act.

At Malacañang Hall where countless numbers of *Rigodon de Honor* were held.
NHI Photo

Filipina stage actor Lea Salonga, the first *Miss Saigon*   *Word.Press.Com photo*

10

The return of Miss Saigon

Miss Saigon, the Broadway musical hit that launched many Filipino thespians' career, including Lea Salonga, the original *Miss Saigon* in 1988, repeats itself by giving another Filipino actor, Laurie Cadevida, a similar boost to her professional career as an international entertainer. Cadevida was recently awarded the prestigious 2007 Helpmann Award (the equivalent of the Tony Award on Broadway), as the best female actor in a musical for her role in the current popular Australian production of *Miss Saigon*, the toast musical show of the 1990s.

This time it was produced in Australia by Michael Coppei & Louise Withers and Associates which, according to a critic, brought to Australian audiences an 'intensely human but heartbreaking love story, whilst dazzling with its technical achievements.' After five weeks of intensive rehearsals in Sydney, the exciting new version was re-staged in Melbourne at Her Majesty's Theatre early this year.

The show was embraced by critics and to popular acclaim: 'Sumptuous, spectacular and sizzling', according to *The Age,* while *The Australian* cited it as 'brilliantly staged and superbly performed.' The opening of *Miss Saigon,* according to *The Sunday Telegraph*, 'works even better – the musical is more real, gritty and intensely emotional than the original show.' *The Sydney Morning Herald* regarded it 'as potent and moving as the original,' while *The Chronicle* said: 'Powerful... thought provoking... beautifully designed piece of musical theatre.' Theatre reviewer Allison Bambridge regarded *Miss Saigon* as 'no feast for the intellect, but the plot is engaging, the staging is effective and it achieves an impressive emotional depth almost effortlessly.' It was also staged in Brisbane from 26 July to 7 September, after breaking box-office records. Again, after its three-months stint at Her Majesty's Theatre in Melbourne, *Miss Saigon* moved to Sydney for an eight week schedule at the Lyric Theatre, Star City, from 20 September to 11 November, 2007.

Filipino expatriates living in Australia, particularly those close to Sydney, could still remember how the first Australian production of *Miss Saigon* was launched at the newly restored Capitol Theatre in the City in 1995. The Australian *Miss Saigon* version was one of the eight versions that were staged after the hit London production that led to performances in Seattle, New York, Los Angeles, Chicago, and later in Germany and other countries in Europe and in Japan, and most recently in Manila. *Miss Saigon* has been seen to date by over 33 million people in over 25 countries, and has been performed in 12 different languages and has won 30 international awards.

The idea of *Miss Saigon* germinated in 1986 when Alain Boublil, the lyricist for *Les Miserables*, and Claude-Michel Schönberg collaborated on a passionate love story of Kim, a young, strong, determined and tough, but honest Vietnemese woman working the bars in Saigon. In the story, she fell in love with an American soldier and soon carried his child. When the Americans were defeated in the Vietnam War, the lovers were separated. The American soldier went back to the US and finally got married to a different woman. The couple was childless. Meanwhile, Kim escaped to Thailand. Thinking of the future of her son, she decided to give her son to an American couple. The musical play, according to its creators, is not a musical story about the Vietnam War. It has a shade of Madame Butterfly in a Vietnam generation setting. The play also symbolises the end of the vision of America as invincible and how it suffered defeat and was brutally humiliated.

The pivotal role of Kim is a difficult one, said to Schönberg during the long search for the actor to play Kim, because aside from being an Asiatic, she is required to sing European music and be able to understand the plot of the story. For almost a year, the search for a performer to play the pivotal role of Kim took the producers to various parts of the world. It ended in Manila towards the end of 1988 when the young Lea Salonga and her childhood friend Monique Wilson, both veterans of the stage Philippine Repertory, captivated the group and decided that they had found Kim in the Philippines.

The two were taken by the producers to London to find out how they would look and project on the stage of the Theatre Royal. Aside from Salonga and Wilson, many budding and veteran Filipino performers were also given an international break. *Miss Saigon* equally opened the door to big opportunities for Isay Alvarez, Pinky Amador, Johnny Amobi, JonJon Briones, Jenine Desiderio, Miguel Diaz, Junix Inocian, Cocoy Laurel, Cornelia Luna, Bobby Martino, Robert Sena, and many others.

The Sydney production of *Miss Saigon* in 1995 also paved the way for many Filipino thespians from the Filipino community. They were given the needed break for their professional careers, like Natalie and Rebecca Jackson Mendoza, Alex Fernandez from Melbourne and Robert Vicencio and Dexter Villahermosa from Sydney. Another batch, composed of Ester Barroso, Cesarh Campos, Genaro G. Lopez, Bobby Martino, Dean Salonga, Christine Sambeli, Rodel San Miguel, Racel Tuazon, Miriam Valmores, Joy Van Uden and Ma-anne Dionisio, was brought in from Manila to strengthen the cast.

The first Kim in Sydney, Joanna Ampil, another Filipino actor who was playing the role of Kim in England after Salonga left the London cast, was brought to Sydney for the role of Kim. Cocoy Laurel completed the cast as The Engineer, 'a fixer, profiteer, a hustler of no fixed morality, race, nationality or language but a survivor.' The search for the right actor to play the complex character of The Engineer was difficult. In the end, they settled initially for Jonathan Pryce, a non-Asian actor. Pryce became the first performer to delineate the role. His looks had to be altered by the magic of make-up. A great transformation of the actor's personality, complete with half-made slit eyes, was seen on the stage when the show opened in London.

When the first Sydney production was decided to be staged at the restored Capitol Theatre, the search was made in Australia and throughout the world for fresh talents. A hundred Filipino aspirants took the audition in Manila and nine of them were brought to Sydney to play various roles, including the coveted role of The Engineer, which went to veteran stage and screen actor and Filipino performer, Cocoy Laurel. He was in the original London cast, playing one of the soldiers. His observation of the character created by Pryce was a learning experience for him. Soon, he was being trained as an understudy for The Engineer's role. Actor Laurel is a scion of a family of politicians and bankers, a truly patriotic clan, but not in the entertainment field, although his father has a good singing voice. Cocoy's grandfather was Jose P. Laurel, the President of the Philippines during the Japanese occupation in the early 1940s, while his father, Salvador C. Laurel, was the vice-president of the Philippines under President Corazon C. Aquino.

A great grandfather of his was one of the signatories to the 1898 Malolos Constitution, the fundamental law of the First Philippine Republic, the first democratic republic in Asia. The eminent lawyer was also a member of the Philippine revolutionary government during the Filipino-American War that ended in 1901. An uncle was a senator, while another was, for a long time, the Speaker of the House of Representatives of the Philippine Congress. Another uncle is a well known banker. The family also owns the Lyceum of the Philippines, one of the most nationalist educational institutions in the country. It was founded by his grandfather.

The youthful looking Filipino actor who has been a performer on stage, screen and recording studio for more than 20 years inherited his talents form his mother, Celia Diaz-Laurel, a veteran theatre actor who had been one of the stalwarts of the Repertory Philippines, the country's leading theatre company. She appears occasionally in local movies, but theatre production is her priority. Actor Laurel has a sister who also sings. His first taste of the limelight was in 1967 when he won a contest to promote Franco Zeffirelli's film *Romeo and Juliet*. Success followed soon after that, not because of his family's political popularity and clout, but rather due to his drama, singing and dancing capabilities. His popularity among his fans was reinforced when he was asked to make a movie, *Lollipops and Roses*, opposite Nora Aunor, then the singing sensation who, like Laurel, developed into a first rate drama actor late in her career. The movie was a great success at the box-office. Movie offers followed and he did some forgettable movies. Recognising the need to hone his craft, Laurel studied acting at the American Academy of Dramatic Arts in New York and studied music composition at the prestigious Julliard School. He also attended dance classes at the Carnegie Hall School. Another talent is portrait painting. He holds a degree in fine arts from the *Academia Real de Bellas Artes* (Academy of Fine Arts) in Madrid. But stage and musical theatre have always been his love and precedence in his career. Like his mother, Laurel is a mainstay in Repertory Philippines production where he played numerous lead roles. Manila theatre goers still remember his creditable and memorable performances in big theatre productions such as *West Side Story, Guys and Dolls, The Elephant Man,* and *Joseph and His Amazing Technicolour Dreamcoat.* But it was his sterling performance in *Les Miserables* that caught the attention of Cameron Macintosh and this paved the way for a fruitful stint in *Miss Saigon* in London in 1989. Laurel was the only original member of the cast of the first London production of *Miss Saigon* who played in the Sydney production. His portrayal of The Engineer's role is not only recognition of his multi-faceted talents but also a confirmation of the talents of Filipinos in the world of musical theatre.

As in 1995, the *Miss Saigon* production which opened in Sydney at the Lyric Theatre, Star City, had three major roles portrayed by Filipino thespians. The role of Kim went to Laurie Cadevida, The Engineer to singer Leo Valdez, now known as Leo Tavorra Valez. Another major role was given to local Filipino talent RJ Rosales who played Thuy, the Vietnamese officer and husband to Kim. Another local talent was Jennifer Trijo who shares the role of Kim in some performances. Both are veterans in musical shows locally. The cast, composed of Filipino talents, was almost universally excellent, with fast-changing sets providing a suitably hectic atmosphere for the action. As in the first Australian *Miss Saigon* production, the second production was dominated by Filipino actors. Aside from the four major roles, there were seven Filipino actors in the cast. They were Rhoda Lopez, Marcus Rivera, Ed Deganos, Jennifer De Leon, Daniel Aguilar, Raymond Balisoro, and Rowena Vilar.

Laurie Cadevida, who played the role of *Miss Saigon,* was born and raised in Los Angeles, California to Filipino parents.

She toured the United States playing the same role and was a veteran of other musical presentations such as *Aida*, the *Pajama Game*, and *Robberbride Groom*. She was a two-time champion on *PAX TX's* Ed McMahon's *Next Big Star* and has performed in LA venues such as the Staple's Centre and Doger Stadium. She has been part of the show for the past two and a half years, beginning right after she celebrated her 18th birthday. It is therefore not surprising that she bagged the coveted annual 2007 Helpmann Award for best musical performer, winning over veteran Divinyls' singer Chrissy Amphlett from *The Boys From Oz* for the best female actor in a musical. The award was named in honour of Sir Robert Helpmann and to commemorate his memory and achievements. It was established in 2001 in Sydney and as mentioned earlier, Australia's answer to Tony Awards on Brodway and the Olivier Awards in London. Cadevida has been noted for her 'strong vocality and a stage presence that truly belies her small stature. She wore the hearts of the audience right from the opening of the show and carried them with her right through to the tragic close.'

Catherine Lambert of *The Daily Telegraph* described the performance of Cadevida as 'fabulous in the heart-wrenching role, with an exceptional voice that she can easily control and she sings with sincerity.' She added that the actor performed with a passion and intensity that shows a depth of understanding about what women endured during the war, so she is convincing and authentic. Another critic said that the actor 'has a sweet, pure voice capable of knocking you back in your seat one moment and drawing you out of it the next.' Yet, another critic said of Cadevida, 'the actor takes us on a truly incredible journey on stage. She is a revelation. *I'd Give My Life For You* is intense and heart wrenching and her duet *I Still Believe* with Katinis sensitively highlights the complexity of these characters.'

Writer Tim Milfull said what others already knew, that the Filipino actor as Kim was 'deeply effective as the innocent girl, forced by necessity into prostitution, hopelessly enamoured of her GI lover and fiercely protective of her baby son, to the point of self-sacrifice in order to relinquish her child to its American father and his new wife.'

Playing understudy of the role of Kim was a young Sydney-sider, Jennifer Trijo, who knows intimately the story of a young mother separated from her child. The 23-year old veteran in local shows in the Filipino community played alternately the role of Kim, the tragic heroine in *Miss Saigon*. Her life experience that guided her performance is drawn from the experience of her mother, Lydia Smith, who left the Philippines to look for greener pastures in Australia. It was only after a year that the two were re-united in Sydney. Replying to a question, Trijo said: 'I am not a mother but I understand this character.' She added: 'I know what is like to be a young Asian immigrant dreaming of a better life.' Trijo's mother made many sacrifices for her family so that they could have a wonderful life in Australia.

Jennifer Trijo was born in Manila, and despite having been raised in Sydney, she is still fluent in her native tongue. *Miss Saigon* was her debut in professional theatre, after winning the panel of judges with her 'raw emotion and natural musical ability.' She has just completed her 3rd year at the University of New South Wales, studying a double degree in Music and Education. She will complete her final year upon completion of the *Miss Saigon* tour. She is also a dedicated chorister and for more than three years an active member of the Collegium Musicum Choir. Outside of her studies, she participates in workshops to further improve her skills, including NIDA's Voice Intensive, and an Alexander Technique

Acting workshop run by David Letch of Screenwise. The young

actor has been involved in community theatre and her credits include: the role of Linda Low in *Flower Drum Song,* and *Bizet's Carmen – the Musical.* She is a veteran in Filipino-Australian community shows, often providing supporting acts to visiting Filipino performers. She recently started to make a name in the Cabaret Circuit: Illawarra Catholic Club; Cabbravale Diggers; and Toukley RSL; she also performed throughout the Eastern Coast of Australia in Corporate and Club performances. She is becoming a role model for young Filipino-Australians. She admitted, that with her income, she could now help her family, who is still living in the Philippines. We learned that she sends money back to the Philippines every week to help put her five cousins through school. 'If I was not fortunate enough to come to this country, I know I would be in their position,' she said in an interview. And added: 'to me it is not a burden to support my family. They are my blood and there is nothing more important that that.'

Another Filipino actor playing a major role in *Miss Saigon* was RJ Rosales, who is playing Thuy, the husband of Kim. He was part of the ensemble for the original Australian *Miss Saigon* production in 1996. He considered that break a major turning point in his life as entertainer; after all, he was a banker with a BS Mathematics degree. Early in his singing career he became a permanent fixture at the SBS Filipino Radio during the time of broadcaster Richie Buenaventura, who recognised his singing talents. For a career decision, he moved to Singapore where he established himself as a much-sought after artist both in theatre and television. He appeared in *Chang and Eng - the Musical,* which brought him to Thailand and Malaysia, performing until 2002. He is also credited for appearing in *The Student Prince, Man of Letters, Cabaret,* and *Forbidden City.* His TV credits include Channel 5's ABC's *Health, Spin* and recently *Style Doctors.*

In the concert scene, he has performed to sell-out concerts at the Jubilee Hall, the Esplanade Concert Hall and at The Waterfront, DBS Theatre and numerous Community Chest Charity Galas. He also appeared in a number of TV and print ads. Prior to coming back to Australia for the *Miss Saigon* role, RJ Rosales had an extensive career in the Philippines, as a singer, actor, host celebrity endorser and recording artist and has worked with the biggest names in the country. He has appeared in numerous TV shows, live concerts and theatre productions, and recorded for various soundtracks. He was last seen in the Manila Metropolitan Film Festival Best Movie for 2005, *Blue Moon* where he was nominated for Best Supporting Actor.

Indeed, *Miss Saigon* is an excellent musical show in all respects, even for non-believers like a particular reviewer who said after seeing a standing ovation from the audience, 'I didn't feel compelled to jump to my feet but I can heartily recommend the show, not just to those who like musicals, but also for theatre goers who would be interested by the more serious notes.' I have seen both the 1995 and current shows and I can say that, even without the helicopter scene – the evacuation of the American embassy and the original show's most memorable scene – the last stage presentation of *Miss Saigon* is captivating and realistic.

The applause was like thunder that echoed and reverberated inside the cavernous His Majesty Theatre in Melbourne when *The American Dream* was performed with gusto by a Filipino actor during the opening of the most awaited return of *Miss Saigon* to Australia. The same accolade was experienced in Brisbane when the show was moved up north for the benefits of theatre goers from the Sunshine state. Now he brings the same gusto and energy in performing the role of The Engineer in *Miss*

Saigon. Of course, I am talking about Filipino singer and stage actor, now known internationally as Leo Tavarro Valdez, taking his maternal family name as part of his stage moniker. ABC Brisbane's Nigel Munro-Wallis, a theatre aficionado and critic, said that the pivotal role of The Engineer played by Tavarro Valdez 'ultimately holds the whole show together' and this is because of the actor's sterling job, bringing his own unique style and stage presence to a difficult role. His performance of the role made another critic to comment that he was 'suitably slimy and unpleasant.' *The Australian* noted that Tavarro Valdez made 'a powerhouse appearance as the Engineer, a venal opportunist.' In fact, the newspaper was amazed how the actor dominated the entire show, drawing everything together in the manner of the MC in another theatre show, *the Cabaret*. Reviewer Allison Bambridge regarded the Filipino actor as the stand-out member for the *Miss Saigon* cast. His portrayal of the character of The Engineer, the sleazy Saigon night club owner and notorious wheeler-dealer, is 'a kind of cockroach character who we admired for his ingenious ability not just to survive but to thrive in these dire circumstances.'

In another review, Brisbane theatre critic, Brett Debritz, said that Tavarro Valdez' portrayal of The Engineer has become synonymous with the flamboyant and charismatic chancer whose selfish machinations drive the story of *Miss Saigon* as one of the world's most popular musicals. In an interview with Tavorra Valdez, he asked the actor to describe his role of The Engineer: "the challenge lies in making The Engineer connect with the audience. He's really a bad guy, but he gets away with the bad thing he does if the audience sees him as a human being as well', he said. 'He was a survivor and survival instinct can make any of us 'do things we normally wouldn't do,' he added. Tavarro Valdez is now very much at ease with the role which he has performed, by the last count, more than 2000 times in five countries. He admitted that he can't help but be fond of 'the character and understanding of his predicament.' Because of this, the actor became the world's foremost interpreter of the character.' Tavarro Valdez started singing at the age of six when he performed 'God Bless You Merry Gentlemen' in a church Christmas program. His mother encouraged him to pursue his singing and shortly he was winning honours at schools for his performances. Without completing his architectural studies at a university, Tavarro Valdez ventured into show business. He became one of the Philippines' best known performers. He was popular on radio, television and in musical theatre. In fact, three times he won the prestigious Best Male Performer Aliw Award, the Philippines' highest entertainment award-giving body. He was also named, three times, as 'one of the most outstanding singers in the country' by the Philippine National Press Club Annual TINIG (voice) Awards. As a singer, he has recorded six albums, three of which have turned gold. He was also popular around Asia. It started when he won the Grand Prize at the first Asian Song Festival. His song *Magsimula Ka* won the best song award and he got the best singer award for his work. He has been used to performing live to huge audiences as a large as 20,000. He travelled and performed in Asia, Europe and America.

The actor's foray into theatre initially as Ravenna in *Armchair*, and the Good God Manama in *Tales of the Mauve*, was appreciated by critics. Both were presented at the Cultural Centre of the Philippines. However, it was at the Metropolitan Theatre that he successfully performed in many musical extravaganzas like *Hindi Kita Malimot, Dahil sa Iyo, Gomburza, Ewagan* and *Sarungbanggi* where the audience honoured the cast with standing ovations at every performance. A turning point in his theatre career came in 1993 when he played the role of Jean Valjean in a repertory Philippines production of *Les Miserables*. It was the same theatre group that honed the raw talents of Lea Salonga, the first *Miss Saigon,* and Monique Wilson, Salonga's understudy for the role of Kim in London. Shortly after the world opening of *Miss Saigon* at Theatre Royal, Drury Lane in London, Jonathan Price, a British actor, played the role of The Engineer for a while. Subsequently, for a year, Tavorra Valdez played the same role in London. Then, in 1995, after Cocoy Laurel who initially played the role of The Engineer left the Australian production, Tavorra Valdez took over the remaining period of the show.

After Sydney, Tavarro Valdez was busy doing concert tours of Asia, Australia and the United States. In 1997, he returned to the show again, playing The Engineer in London until 1999, at which time he became involved in the *Miss Saigon* tour of the Far East (Manila, Hong Kong and Singapore) for a year. Then, for the next two years he was on a UK National tour by the *Miss Saigon* cast. His experience was finally recognised by his peers in the industry when he was honoured in the Philippines with a Life Achievement Award in the field of Performing Arts. This actor was not only busy with his theatre and singing activities, he also found time to engage in charity fund-raisers for the church or civic minded groups providing help to the under-privileged.

When *Miss Saigon* was to be re-staged in Australia, Cameron Macintosh had only one person in mind to play The Engineer – that was Tavarro Valdez. After long years of involvement with *Miss Saigon,* the actor considers the show as a major part of 'his life, not merely a career, but his whole life.'

Gems of thought of
Pura Santillan-Castrence

The Filipino, in general, believes in abstractions but fails to face reality which exacts justice and integrity. This is the reason why bribery goes on, and so does *lagay* and every other forms of dishonesty.

*****

Many Filipinos are what I call Sunday – religious, that is, they go to church every Sunday, take in confession and communion, but the rest of the week they bribe and do corrupt deeds, the way corruption is practised in many parts of the world.

*****

Only the strong, unrelenting efforts of Filipino people can erase the blemishes in our culture and remove the negative label attached to it. Fortunately, there are concerned Filipinos who, with all their might, attack 'these cultural damages' with the pen and with the tongue. They are unrelenting.

*****

Reading books may also lead to the acquisiton of wisdom. Filipinos, although they care for education, generally do not love books. They read up on materials relating to their specific field of study, but eschew everything else.

11

The passing of a great Filipina

I have been fortunate in my career as historical researcher and a lover of history to have established friendships and acquaintances with persons who in their lives and career contributed so much to the country of my birth. I am referring to distinguished Filipinos like national historian and university Professor Teodoro T. Agoncillo, editor and ambassador Emilio Aguilar Cruz, man of medicine and historian Dr. Domingo Abella, Rizalist Dr. Sixto Roxas, historian Fr. Horacio de la Costa, and another avid Rizalist and historian Professor Esteban A. de Ocampo, who in many ways influenced my interest in historical research and the things we normally take for granted, our cultural heritage. These people are now gone but they left individual legacies that every Filipino should be thankful for.

Another person whom I admired and respected most because of her contribution to Filipino cultural heritage and untiring concern of what would become of 'the old country' – the Philippines. I am referring to a great lady whose imprint in Philippine literature, journalism and diplomatic history of the Philippines will always remind us how to be a true Filipino. She passed away, at the ripe age of 101, on 15 January 2007, less than a couple of weeks before her 102nd birthday.

I was scheduled to pay her a visit in November of that year. This lady whom I learned to admire, love, and care about because of her humility, in spite of her fame and achievements, became a close friend, although we lived apart, she in Melbourne and myself in Sydney. In the same year she died, her whole life contribution to the 'old country' was scheduled to be acknowledged by a grateful nation when the National Commission for Culture and the Arts conferred on her the *Dangal ng Haraya* Life Achievement Award. To me it is not a posthumous award, because two weeks before she died she was informed of the NCCA award. In fact, she decided to send her acceptance of the award through me without knowing that she would not be able to feel the medallion and hear the reading of her citation recognizing what she had done for her country.

The last time I saw her in person was when she celebrated her 100th birthday in 2005. After that important event, we continued our communication, mostly through telephone. I enjoyed the exchange of ideas with her, particularly in discussions about her column in the *Bayanihan News*, an Australia-wide newspaper in the Filipino community.

I could still remember a piece she wrote, and how she further explained to me the importance of the details that she wanted to impart to her readers. After a couple of hours discussion, I realized and understood why she never applied for Australian citizenship but continued to be a Filipino citizen until her death. She had an undying love for her country.

I am talking about an incident in her life during the Japanese occupation which was mentioned in the article, titled 'Need and Response'. She was already starting a diplomatic career then at was what to become the Department of Foreign Affairs in the Ermita district of Manila. Outside her work hours, she would teach the French language at the old UP Padre Faura. She told me that after her teaching work, she would walk home, but instead of using the shorter route, she would take the longer route because she avoided the street corners. I asked why and she told me that at every corner of the shorter route Japanese soldiers were assigned to man a sentry to whom Filipinos were obliged to bow. She said that she would rather walk an extra mile than make a bow to foreign forces occupying her own country. She admitted that it was her way of doing a Gandhi-style peaceful civil disobedience, which she consciously practiced. As a friend and admirer, it was a privilege that I could attend her 100th birthday, a milestone in her life. For me it was an honour to be counted as one of her closest friends, and personally introduced to the Castrence family. Four of her children came to celebrate her birthday, with so many of her grandchildren living in Australia. Son Ricardo, who was in the Philippines, and another daughter Sylvia who was in the United States, rang their mother to greet the grand lady on that important day.

Pura Santillan-Castrence's works were known to me when I was still working in the Philippines as a cultural administrator and historical researcher for the National Historical Institute (NHI). The NHI was headed then by Professor Esteban A. de Ocampo, a *balae* of her, being the father of Ambassador Susan Castrence, wife to Ricardo Castrence, her youngest son.

I am also familiar with many of her English essays that appeared in the *Philippine Prose and Poetry*, a text book series used in high school English classes in the Philippines. Her essays were one of my few favourite literary works written in the English language, mainly because of her writing style.

It was in the early 1980s – having already retired from government service – that I met the author in person. She was then doing translation work for the NHI. When I migrated to Australia in late 1988, I became acquainted with her again through the defunct *The Filipino Herald*, a newspaper in theFilipino community in Sydney, where we both wrote articles.

When the *Bayanihan News* started publication in 1999, Castrence was commissioned by its editor and publisher to write articles exclusive to the newspaper because her other essays were already being syndicated then in the United States and also in a couple of newspapers in Australia.

She was already 94 years old and had a handicap being blind and hard of hearing, but agreed to contribute newly written materials to the *Bayanihan News*. The newspaper was developing its own readership, particularly those not familiar with her writings. I was surprised to know that even in the autumn period of her life, she maintained a unique way of interpreting contemporary events and the events that happened before that she still vividly remembered. I particularly enjoyed talking with her when she would ring me or I rang her to discuss the articles she sent the newspaper. The only hindrance from her producing more articles during the five years she was writing for this newspaper was the fact that she was legally blind and hard of hearing.

Fortunately, Gina Lytras, her caregiver, agreed to help take dictation of articles she wanted to share with the readers of this newspaper. That collaboration lasted until early 2006 when her articles were published in book form. To me, the publication of this compilation of her articles highlighted her late writing career. The book took the title of her column and became *As I See It: Filipinos and the Philippines*.

Her admirers welcomed the new publication. One contemporary admirer said: 'Her insights may be simplistic but they serve to ignite the continuing debate on what ails the Philippine society.' It was also observed that her writings are redolent of her nationalist sentiments and her unwavering faith in the Filipino.

Professor Randy David praised the compilation of her latest

work and said: 'The standpoint from which Pura Santillan-Castrence writes about her country is unique. She is 100-years old, lives abroad, and has been blind for many years. Yet she writes from a powerful memory and an unerring insight. She writes about the Philippines with the nostalgia of a native who has known a gentler time, and with the wisdom of a seer who has glimpsed the future.'

Another member of the academe, Dr. Mina Roces of the School of History, University of New South Wales in Sydney, regarded her book as 'human story where a self-reflexive 100 year old woman touches the reader with her own assessment of her career, education and parenthood. It is also an important book because the author (who was a suffragist) captures snippets of life in the Philippines before the war and gives us first hand accounts of what the Manila Carnival was like, or how teachers and parents decided one's choices in life. These accounts of pre-War Philippines are rare and valuable for historians and Filipinists interested in narratives of the past.'

Yet another admirer of Dr. Castrence, Dr. Nicanor G. Tiongson, Dean of the College of Mass Communication, University of the Philippines, said: 'On her 100th birthday, there can be no better tribute to Pura Santillan-Castrence, pioneering feminist and respected writer, than the publication of her most recent columns, many of which are valuable eyewitness accounts of events and personalities decisive in Philippne history. Furthermore, the book is eloquent proof that the human mind and will can triumph over age and physical disability in order to impart to a younger generation of Filipinos insights gleaned from a life lived fully and well.' Indeed, the compilation of her last literary pieces captured what a biographer said in the late 1960s, when she described Castrence's literary merits as of a person with a 'writer's maturity, richness of background and experience, a philosophy of life and a style that is forceful and flexible.'

Pura Santillan-Castrence was born in Sta. Mesa, Manila on 24 March 1905 to Gregorio Santillan and Encarnacion Sandiko. She spent her early childhood in Bulacan but obtained her elementary and high school education in Manila's public school system. A product of the University of the Philippines, she completed her B.S. in Pharmacy in 1925 and her M.A. in Chemistry in 1929. She went on to further her study, as a Barbour Scholar for her Doctor of Philosophy degree at the University of Michigan concentrating on language studies. Returning to the Philippines, she resumed her teaching post at the State University

She was a linguist and at ease in Spanish, French, German, Italian, and English, and of course, her Tagalog dialect. As a writer in English, Castrence was named 'Most Outstanding Filipino Woman writer in English in 1949' by the Civic Assembly of Women and 'Most distinguished Writer of 1957' by the Far Eastern University. Other important citations and awards followed. She was awarded a Smith-Mundt Leadership grant in 1957 and membership in the most prestigious *Akademya ng Wikang Pambansa*.

As a diplomat, she was one of the pioneer career diplomats in the Office of Foreign Relations, in fact the first woman Minister. She rose to higher positions in the department due to her work and commitment. Soon, she became the Minister-counsellor in Germany, and finally the position of Assistant Secretary for Cultural Affairs and Information, with the rank of ambassador, until her retirement from government service in the 1970s.

No doubt that, as a writer, Castrence injected quality into her writings to a high degree. In 1967, a short biography of her appeared in *Women of Distinction* and her biographer, Conchita

Faustino-Villena, talked about the merits of her literary works and said: 'As an essayist, she injects the quality of life-likeness in her works to a high degree. It is she who gives the norm and standard, not of art, but of reality. Because of this realism, her works have left an imprint on the social life of the Filipinos, especially on the women. As a columnist, she makes her columns reflect the ever changing attitude of the fleeting present, and as such, they are interesting as they apply to issues current at that time they were written. Her columns, conducted within the bounds of journalistic tenets, do a lot of good for the general welfare besides being rich fountains of entertainment, humour, and pleasant reading. She has the writer's maturity, the richness of background and experience, a philosophy of life, and a style that is forceful and flexible. As a critic, she has done much for the public welfare, for she has a deep social consciousness. As a writer, she is fearless in exposing the evils and corruption of the times and is brave to call the attention of the public to things and places that need to improve.' This accolade was written in late 1967 when she was only 62. One could therefore imagine the volume of work she produced during the next four decades until her death.

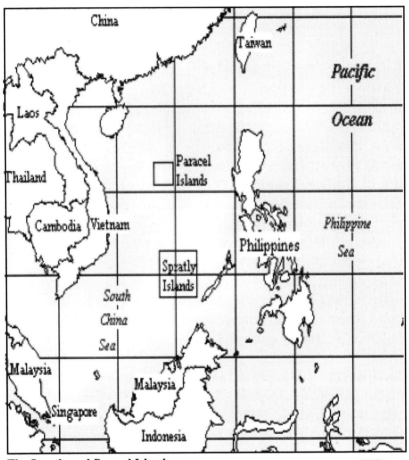

The Spratly and Paracel Islands

12

Territorial claims

The Spratly Islands issue

'It is obvious from the Treaty that the Paracels and the Spratlys were not ceded to any country but are subject to the disposition of the Allies in the last World War. By no means, therefore, can any single country acquire sovereignty over the Paracels and the Spratlys by the use or display of force in the vicinity. Therefore, we regret to say that such an act would be in violation of international law as well as the Charter of the United Nations.'
- General Carlos P. Romulo.

The Spratly Islands problem resurfaced as one of the controversial issues haunting the Arroyo government in connection with its dealing with China. It looks like the government is caught in a quicksand that is slowly pulling it down, beyond salvation. Many are aware of 'Hello Garci', the fertiliser scam, and most recently the NBN-ZTE controversies. Now it is for the Spratlys to be in the forefront of controversies that the administration wishes to disappear, but it resurfaces via a contract signed by the Arroyo Government with China and Vietnam to undertake a joint seismic study in the disputed Spratly islands. But according to political observers the contract that was signed also included a part of the country's area of jurisdiction. Critics are accusing the action of Arroyo as unconstitutional and serious grounds for impeachment.

Why is the Spratlys important to the Philippines?

The *Sydney Morning Herald* reported in 1995 that the group of islets and reefs, commonly known as Sprawls, believed 'to be rich in oil and natural gas deposits and bruited about as the next Middle East, could be the next point of conflict in the Asia-Pacific region, particularly so that China is adamant in its claim of territorial jurisdiction over 80% of the South China Sea. Recent Chinese official statements confirmed that the Nash islands, as they called the Spratlys, have been inhabited by them since time immemorial.

Australia, like any country in the region, was alarmed at China's position on the controversy, which is a total claim to almost the entire South China Sea and an accompanying military build-up in the islands would allow China to dominate the area. It added that any action in the South China Sea could result in increased tension in the whole Asia-Pacific region. The South China Sea is one of the busiest sea routes in the region.

The Spratlys issue has already brought tension among the members of ASEAN, particularly among Brunei, Malaysia, the Philippines and Vietnam, all claiming territorial jurisdiction in whole or part over the islands, not to mention Taiwan's claim over the area too. China's claim of 5.1 million square kilometres of sea cut across Malaysia's gas fields off Sarawak, some Vietnamese oil discoveries, part of the 200km of territorial sea of the Philippines, and part of the Natuna gas field of Indonesia. The meeting held in Manila in late 1998 underscored the importance of resolving the issue for the peace and security of the region. The tension between countries in the region caused a diplomatic row between China and the Philippines in 1994, with the latter lodging a formal diplomatic protest over the movement of Chinese military men to the islands. Most recently, separate incidents involving Malaysian forces vs. Filipino naval forces and Vietnamese forces vs. Philippine air force elements further confirmed the tension over the Spratlys.

A couple of years ago, the Australian press reported that China's determination to eventually gobble up the entire disputed area is evident in the construction of 8 Chinese military structures on Mischief Reef, part of the Spratlys which the Philippines claimed in 1978 and called the *Kalayaan* (Freedom) Islands Group. Mishief Reef is east of the Philippines' Palawan Island and 650 nautical miles from China's southern island of Hainan. There have been no less than 30 outposts constructed on these South China Sea islands over the past few years by five of the claimant countries.

In the Philippines, the Spratly Islands came to prominence when, in 1956, a successful lawyer-businessman, known to many as 'Vice-Admiral' Tomas Cloma, Sr., issued an open notice to the world about his claim to the group of islands, islets, coral reefs, shoals, and sand cays comprised within what he called *Freedomland* and the nearby seven-island group, the Spratly islands. He said he discovered the islands during many fishing expeditions to the South China Sea between 1947 and 1956. Tomas Cloma, Sr., was born in Panglao, Bohol in the Visayas, on 18 September 1904 to Spanish settler Ciriaco Cloma and a Bohol-born maiden, Irena Arbolente. An adventurer by nature, he went to Manila at the age of 15 years and worked his way to complete his high school education at the Arellano High School in Tondo, Manila. Subsequently, he worked for the Manila Railroad Company, now the Philippine National Railways, at its main Tutuban station. It was at the railway company that he became a licensed telegraph operator. This new qualification brought him to San Fernando, La Union, north of Manila, where he was assigned. It was there that he met lovely Victoria Luz Borromeo Galves, who later became his wife.

To further the education of the newly weds, the couple decided to move back to Manila where Victoria took a course in nursing, while he pursued his law degree at the Far Eastern University while working for the *Manila Bulletin*, a national newspaper. He worked as assistant editor of the shipping section of the *Bulletin* and was also assigned to cover the Senate and labour beats where he made friends with influential people who helped him achieve his life ambition–to go back to his roots in Bohol as an accomplished man. A business minded person, he established the *Commercial Information Service* which published a shipping manifesto for all incoming and outgoing cargoes in the Philippines. Later, he formed the Dagohoy Trading Shipping Company, consisting of passenger sailboats ferrying people on oversized outriggers from Lucena in Quezon province, and the Visayas. The Visayas Fish Corporation came later. Another interest during this period was a successful lighterage business with three tugboats plying the Pasig River.

The increase in the number of tugboats he operated resulted in the idea of a private nautical school, based in Manila. The Philippine Maritime Institute, popularly known today as PMI College, was established by Cloma in 1948, with 25 students on a lonely barge docked along the Pasig River behind the old PLDT building, Magallanes Drive, Intramuros, Manila. From a small group of students in 1948, the PMI College was granted recognition by the Department of Education in 1950. It expanded and most recently recorded an enrolment of more than 25,000 students spread throughout its three campuses in Manila, Quezon City and Tagbilaran City in Bohol province, and became the biggest nautical school in the Philippines.

Fondly called by friends and admirers as 'Admiral', Tomas

Cloma's important role in contemporary history, came when in one of his fishing expeditions in the later 1940s, he 'discovered' a batch of uninhabited islands and newly emerged reefs just off Palawan in the South China Sea. The location was a rich fishing ground. The idea of claiming the islands was discussed with his friends, such as the late Philippine President and Foreign Affairs Secretary Carlos P. Garcia, a fellow Boholano, and Senator Lorenzo Tañada. He called the islands *The Free Territory of Freedomland*. In 1956, he filed an open notice to the world at the United Nations to signify his intentions and stated that Filipino settlers occupied some of the islands and governed themselves according to Filipino customs and traditions under Philippine laws. A few problems with other foreign troops were, however, experienced by the settlers, mainly Vietnamese and Taiwanese forces.

In 1972, when Martial Law was declared in the Philippines, 'Admiral' Tomas Cloma was imprisoned for 'impersonating a military officer by being called an 'admiral'. For four months, he languished in jail and eventually gave up his personal claim over the islands he discovered. With that decision went all his documentation and films including a film showing the raising of the first flag on the main island of Freedomland. In 1978, then President Ferdinand Marcos issued a decree declaring the islands as part of the Philippines and giving them the name *Kalayaan* (Freedom). Although Cloma relinquished his claim over the Spratly islands group, he pursued to the very end his claim of ownership over the rest of *Freedomland*, near the disputed islands, which he agreed with the Philippine government interpretation that for all purposes are *res nullius*, meaning belonging to no one and only subject to modes of acquisition under international law such as territorial discovery and occupation. Tomas Cloma's contributions to Philippine contemporary history was finally recognised by the government in December 1995, while tension was already escalating in the area, when then Philippine President Fidel V. Ramos presented the ailing Cloma with the Legion of Honour, the highest military award given to a civilian for outstanding services to the Philippines. Cloma died in 1996 at the age of 92.

Now back to the disputed Spratly islands. In 1956, Cloma wrote to the Philippine government concerning his group's activities undertaking survey and occupation work 'in a territory in the China Sea outside of Philippines waters and that his group was claiming ownership of the 'unoccupied' territory based on 'the rights of discovery and/or occupation.' Subsequently, Cloma established a separate government for the *Free Territory of Freedomland* and requested a 'protectorate' status of the islands from the Republic of the Philippines. In an official reply to Cloma, the Philippine government, through then Vice-President and Foreign Affairs Secretary Carlos P. Garcia, stated that it regards Cloma's Freedomland as *res nullius* but clarified the status of the seven-island group known internationally as the Spratlys. The Philippine Government told Cloma that 'the government considers these islands as under the *de facto* trusteeship of the victorious Allied Powers of the Second World War, as a result of the Japanese Peace Treaty, signed and concluded in San Francisco, on 8 September 1951, where Japan renounced all its rights, title and claim over the Spratly islands and to the Paracel Islands, and there being no territorial settlement made by the Allied Powers, up to the present with respect to their disposition. It follows, therefore, that as long as this group of islands remain in that status, it is equally open to economic exploitation and settlement by nationals of any member of the Allied Powers on the basis of equality of opportunity and treatment in social, economic and commercial matters relating thereto.' The Foreign Affairs Department added that the Philippines is one of the Allied Powers which defeated Japan in the Second World War, and is also a signatory power to the Japanese Peace Treaty.

The importance of the Spratly islands and islets, which compose only one-sixth of the entire area of 80,000 square nautical miles, to the security of the Philippines was already evident in the last part of Garcia's statement in the 1950s when he said: 'In view of the geographical location of these group of islands and islets embraced within *Freedomland*, their proximity to the western territorial boundaries of the Philippines, their historical and geological relations to the Philippine archipelago, their immense strategic value to our national defence and security, aside from their economic potential which is admittedly considerable in fishing, coral and sea products, and in rock phosphate, assuredly the Philippine Government does not regard with indifference the economic exploitation and settlement of these uninhabited and unoccupied groups of islands and islets by Philippine nationals so long as they are engaged in furtherance of their legitimate pursuits.'

Philippine policy on the Spratlys islands was clearly manifested when the Philippine government sent notes to Manila's Embassies on the Republic of China and Republic of Vietnam in 1972 stating that the Kalayaan group, sometimes referred to as the Spratlys, 'had been acquired by right of occupation [by the Philippines]...' Commenting on the issue, the late General Carlos P. Romulo said in 1972 that:

'the Philippines has every right to feel the necessity to securing this area (Spratlys) for its protection. 'In the Treaty of Peace with Japan, signed in San Francisco in 1951, the following provision is mentioned with respect to the Paracels and the Spratlys: '(f) Japan renounces all rights, title and claims to the Spratly Islands and to the Paracel Islands,' (Article 2 of the treaty). ... it is obvious from the Treaty that the Paracel and the Spratlys were not ceded to any country but are subject to the disposition of the Allies in the last World War. By no means, therefore, can any single country acquire sovereignty over the Paracels and the Spratlys by the use of display of force in the vicinity therefore. We regret to say that such an act would be in violation of International Law as well as the Charter of the United Nations.'

The Sabah claim

One of the recent decisions of the Arroyo government that remained mainly unnoticed by the general public was the revival of the so-called 'Sabah Desk' in the Department of Foreign Affairs. The Foreign Affairs Department spokesman said that the decision was related to the ongoing negotiation to open a Philippine consulate in Sabah and the status of many Filipino migrants in that part of East Malaysia. This decision, however, did not escape the eagle eye of the Sultan of Sulu, who claims proprietary rights to Sabah. He cautioned the government to be transparent in dealing with Malaysia on whatever agreement it is negotiating that might affect the Philippine claim to the territory. In a statement issued by his Interim Supreme Royal Ruling Council, Jamalul Kiram III, it was revealed that he will not recognize any agreement reached by the two countries concerning the Sabah issue. He added that he issued royal decrees asking his constituents to follow his decrees. The Sultan felt that the Sultanate had again left in the dark as to what political leverage the Arroyo government will use in negotiating with Malaysia concerning the Sabah claim, which was initiated by her late father, President Diosdado Macapagal in 1962. Kiram also revealed that technically the Philippine government no longer has the authority to pursue the claim since he revoked in 1989 the special power of attorney granted by his predecessor to the Macapagal administration in 1962.

The Philippine claim to Sabah, according to Michael Leifer, an academic who made an exhaustive study of the Sabah claim, has attracted 'more notoriety than serious attention outside of these islands [Philippines].' He reasoned out that it was because of the 'air of political improvisation and private greed which has surrounded the presentation of the claim' that, he believed, tended to detract from the justification of the claim.

Records show that the Sultan of Sulu was the sovereign of Sabah, part of North Borneo as early as the 17th century. He retained his sovereignty over the territory until the late 1950s, when he signed a special power of attorney granting the Philippine government the rights to pursue the case. Looking back further before this, records tell us that the Sultan of Sulu come into possession of most of North Borneo in 1704 when the Sultan of Brunei disposed of the territory east of the Kimanis river as reward for the military assistance rendered by Sulu to the Brunei Sultanate in a war against its enemy.

In 1878, Mohammed Jamalul Alam, Sultan of Sulu, leased or ceded the territory in the North East of the island of Borneo to Gustavus Baron de Overbeck and Alfred Dent. In consideration of the lease or cession [conflicting definition of the term 'padjak' by both sides], the Sultan was to receive annually the sum of five thousand Straits dollars. In 1903, an additional three hundred dollars was agreed and added to the financial agreement. In 1881, the British North Borneo Company was incorporated upon application to the British Crown by Overbeck and Dent and became the administrator of North Borneo. Eventually the territory became a British Protectorate. In 1946 its status was changed to a British Colony.

The official interest of the Philippines over the territory is said to have started in that year when its ambassador in London was directed to obtain copies of the agreement between the North Borneo Company and the British Crown concerning the transfer of the sovereign rights and assets of the chartered company to the British government. According to Leifer, the transfer of sovereign rights happened at the very time the Philippines was granted its independence by the United States of America. He added that the proclamation 'marked an attempt [on the part of the British government] to forestall any claim [over Sabah] from the new government in Manila.' Ambassador Armando Manalo regarded the British action as 'an act of naked political aggrandizement in the widely discredited imperialist tradition.' Former American governor-general of the Philippines Francis Burton Harrison, even described the annexation by the British as 'political aggression.' Harrison urged the Philippine government then to take action.

In the late 1950s, the Sultan of Sulu abrogated the 1878 Deed and he executed an Instrument ceding the territory of North Borneo to the Philippines. The situation was muddled when, in the early 1960s, the British government announced, through the government of Malaya, that the Borneo territories would be included in a new Federation of Malaysia. The Philippine government protested and severed its diplomatic relations with Malaya and it withheld recognition of the Federation. The issue reached a stalemate when both countries adopted opposing views concerning their positions over the Sabah issued. Malaysia's position is no claim, while the Philippines brings the case to the International Court of Justice. Ambassador Manalo said in the late 1960s: 'Malaysia's unyielding and inflexible stand on the Sabah issue suggests that perhaps the answers to these questions are not entirely favorable to it. In contrast to Malaysia's obduracy, the Philippines has emphasized its willingness to try all peaceful means, in keeping with the Manila Accord, of resolving a disagreement that already has raised discordant notes of tension in a corner of the world that can least afford conflict....'

This is the scenario when the incumbent government revives its interest over the Sabah claim. Will President Gloria Arroyo follow her father's decision concerning the claim, which Michael Leifer described as 'political improvisation' given the current situation facing her administration? In a paper delivered at a conference on the subject, Professor Rolando N. Quintos, a historian and scholar, said that the only way to break the deadlock between the Philippines and Malaysia on the Sabah claim is through a give and take approach. He said, 'Let the Philippines be willing to accept the justice of the Malaysian appeal to self-determination and accept the final conclusion of the UN Secretary General of September 1963, if, in return, the Malaysians are willing to submit the purely legal claim of the Philippines in support of the proprietary rights of the Kiram heirs in Sabah to the World Court or to a mutually acceptable mediating body.'

Eva Peron   The Bettmann Archive

Imelda R. Marcos   NHI Photo

Eva Peron at the Opera   Anna Scarpa Photo

**Imelda R. Marcos at the Sydney
Opera House Opening**   NHI Photo

13

Two women: Evita and Imelda

A few years back, anyone who saw the movie *Evita*, the Madonna and Antonio Banderas film, is reminded of another familiar woman character whose life has an uncanny resemblance to the legendary former First Lady of Argentina, Evita Peron, the subject of the Golden Globe Award winning film.

'I am not a prostitute', this was the reaction of Imelda Marcos, then the First Lady and the most powerful woman in the Philippines, when informed about the obvious comparison between her and Evita Peron.

The analogy between the two female partners of two of the worlds best known dictators surfaced during the confrontation with the late Senator Benigno Aquino, privy to Imelda's *declass past*. In attacking Imelda for her expensive Cultural Centre of the Philippines construction project, Senator Aquino observed that it was ludicrous for a poor country like the Philippines to build such an expensive monument. During the heated controversy, the senator suggested that Imelda's building complex is traceable to an impoverished childhood similar to that of Evita Peron.

In the unauthorised biography of Imelda Marcos, *Imelda: Steel Butterfly of the Philippines,* authored by Catherine Ellison, it was said that 'Aquino's comparison was valid even aside from the obvious parallel between the two women's ascents from squalor to vast power and wealth. Both had developed constant themes concerning how much she loved and worked for the masses, how she hated her country's privileged 'oligarchy', and how well she complemented her husband, of whom Evita once said, in phrases redolent of Imelda, 'in different ways we had both wanted to do the same thing: he with intelligence, I with the heart... he master and I pupil'. In 1970, the Philippine propaganda machinery said about the Marcoses: 'Ferdinand would be the brain; Imelda would be the heart. Ferdinand would build the body; Imelda would provide it with a soul'. The image of an ideal partnership was created–he as impersonal, unsentimental and with a heart of steel and she as caring and concerned with the finer aspects of life–'the true and the good and the beautiful.'

Like Imelda, Evita Peron had a humble beginning and a childhood that she wanted to be forgotten or erased. Both have their own official biographies stating very little of their early growing up years. In 1919, Eva Maria Ibarguren, an illegitimate child, was born to Juana Ibarguren, the mistress of Juan Duarte. Her father was an important man in the community. But everyone knew that he was married to Estela Grisolia and had three daughters by her. As the second woman, Juana gave him five children, four girls and a boy; Evita was the youngest. A year after her birth, her father left the family and returned to his 'real family' leaving Evita's mother working alone and barely surviving to feed her five children. Evita was too young to understand the departure of her father. However, the family experience during the funeral of her father, who died when she was seven, had an effect on her mind. It opened her eyes to the reality that they were outcasts. Initially, because they were illegitimate children, they were barred during the wake from seeing their father for the last time. A heated argument between the two families of the deceased ensued; however, in the end the outcasts were allowed a last glimpse of their father and permitted to accompany the coffin to the cemetery but tailing a distance behind the procession.

Imelda Marcos was born in 1929, ten years after Evita's birth. Although her parents were legally married, her mother was the second wife of Orestes Vicente Romualdez who had five children by his first wife. Her father's branch of the Romualdez family was the poorest. Five children were born after. Early in life after the death of her mother, Imelda cared for her siblings. She was closest to brother Benjamin, who like Evita's brother, Juan, played an important part in her political life. Benjamin, nicknamed Kokoy, became Philippine ambassador to the US. He was Imelda's spy and trouble shooter in Washington while Juan Duerte served as presidential secretary to President Juan Domingo Peron. Both men contributed to the legend of Imelda Marcos and the myth of Evita Peron, respectively.

While Evita had little education, Imelda attended a catholic school and completed a college degree in education. However, fearing of boredom in a teaching career and a dreary life in a little provincial city where her dream lifestyles could not be fulfilled, Imelda left her birthplace with a small suitcase, few clothes and 5 pesos, about $2.50 at that time, in her purse.

In similar circumstances, Evita's family left the shame and insecurity of Los Toldos, her birth place. She was twelve when they settled in Junin, a small city whose residents looked at Buenos Aires with dreams and fantasies. At fifteen, Evita left her family and braved the adverse conditions in the city to pursue her ambition to become an actor. With no money, little education and questionable talents, she wanted to prove that she could conquer a city and become a star. Her life in the city was vague. It is not clear how she initially survived. She had a small radio job, entered and lost a beauty contest, and she presided over a tango dance contest, the latest craze of the time. From small radio roles she became a movie extra, then given either non-speaking or otherwise minor parts on stage.

She lived for six months with a young actor in 'a real apartment, a home with furniture and everything, a real life, a decent life', but the relationship was short-lived. The man took a new partner and Evita was left alone without security for the future. During her first few years in the big city, she changed the way she dressed and presented herself to the world. Her bitterness and desire to avoid humiliation had toughened and improved her perspective in life. For 10 years, her hunt for the elusive break in the entertainment industry was bleak and trivial. Later gossip about this period in her life alluded to her refutations as a *putita* who slept around for radio parts. By 1939, she became quite successful. Her first big contract came in 1943. It was a chance of a lifetime but which brought her little security through portraying the characters of Elizabeth I, Catherine the Great, Alexandra of Russia, Carlota of Mexico, Sarah Bernhardt, and others. She became one of the best-paid actresses in Buenos Aires. After 6 years in the city, at the age of twenty three she met a forty eight year old younger-looking widower, Colonel Juan Domingo Peron, a man taller than most Argentinians. He had a muscular build, with a wide face, blackhair combed back and plastered down. He had a so-called 'movie actor's' smile, a wide mouth and white teeth, and, almost savage appearance – a masculine man in a country where there is a 'cult of masculinity.' During that first meeting with Evita, Colonel Peron was smitten by her fragile look, strong voice, long blonde hair falling loose to her back, and fevered eyes. His enemies regarded Peron as a Nazi, a tyrant, a bungler, an embezzler, and a child molester. But to his admirer, he was a generous, gregarious, and a sexually attractive man, a brilliant teacher and intellectual, a good judge of men and a political genius. By this time, Evita never talked of her past. She guarded her secret effectively. She avoided any discussion of the subject publicly and bridled awkward questions. Her early life was never mentioned in official circles, or else it was romanticised in ambiguous terms.

Having a degree in education was no passport to a better life. Imelda left the province and arrived in the city as one of the refugees from rural poverty. She lived in her cousin's mansion on the outskirts of Manila. She occupied a room in the servant's quarters. Her cousin was a congressman and his wife was a haughty woman who assigned Imelda the task of running errands and caring for the adopted three young girls. As promised, her cousin eventually found Imelda's first job at a music store in Escolta, Manila. As a sales clerk, she demonstrated the piano to prospective customers and accompanied her sales strategy with songs. The provincial songbird attracted many on-lookers. It was there that she met Benigno Aquino, a shorter, skinny, and bespectacled young man who courted her. The courtship was dismissed as a mere flirtation. No serious attachment developed. Aquino became her political enemy thirty years later. Imelda first tasted popularity in the city when she landed on the cover of a Valentine issue of *This Week*, a widely circulated magazine of *The Manila Chronicle*. Her 'regal bearing and heart-shaped face' was admired by countless readers of the magazine nationwide. A more prestigious job was found for her at the Central Bank of the Philippines. She worked as a clerk. She became popular among her co-employees as the provincial 'beauty queen' who sang during lunch breaks. After office hours, she would attend the Philippine Women's University College of Music and Arts where she was enrolled on a scholarship. Her teacher admired her fine mezzo-soprano voice and considered her as talented. Her beauty and training brought her to the *Miss Manila Beauty* competition whose winner would represent Manila during the *Miss Philippine* competition, but she failed to reach the group of finalists chosen by a board. The defeat was a challenge and she protested the decision and personally appealed her case to Manila's City Mayor, Arsenio Lacson. The mayor was known for his reputation of helping distressed pretty young women in need of favours. After the meeting with Mayor Lacson, where Imelda was reported to have blinking tears in her eyes while appealing her case, the well known dashing lothario disowned the board's choice and selected Imelda Romualdez as Manila's official candidate to the *Miss Philippine* contest.

Controversy followed when the board overruled the mayor's decision; in the end she was given a consolation title of *Muse of Manila*. This incident resulted in gossip circulating around town that she got the title by seducing the mayor. The scandal was only the first among the many scandals that would colour Imelda's life, including the liaison with a scion of a prominent and wealthy Manila family, but a married man. Many men have been linked with Imelda, even while she was still in the province. There was a lumberyard owner, an electric company head, a basketball player, a Protestant physician, and a bona fide member of an elite family – the son of a cabinet secretary. It was rumoured too that the beauty title she owned attracted a screen test at the Sampaguita film studio, one of the biggest film companies in the Philippines at that time, but the Romualdez family looked down on acting as a profession. It could have been a passport to instant popularity as what happened to Evita Peron in Argentina.

In 1954, Evita Peron was already dead when Imelda met a young politician named Ferdinand Marcos. He was an ambitious, aggressive, successful and controversial second-term member of the Philippine Congress. It was a love at first sight, gifts of rose buds and walks under pine trees followed. The 11-day romance which ended in a secret wedding in City of Baguio was the subject of a society page headline. Imelda was on her way to greatness and realisation of her ambition. The man she married was to become the most maligned and hated president of the Philippines.

In their respective lives as women partners of heads of state, Evita and Imelda attracted countless controversies for every move they made. Their shopping appetites were known, not only among local social circles in Argentina and the Philippines, but throughout the world.

When Evita, with her mother, went to Ricciardi, the best jeweller in Buenos Aires, the store, it was reported, was cleared by her body guards of its customers for the two women to shop. They received special prices, but later, when Evita's payment was delayed, Ricciardi took to hiding his best stones whenever it was announced that Evita intended to visit his shop.

Imelda's obsession to shop where she spent millions of dollars disregarding the serious economic condition in the Philippines was known. In *The Rise and Fall of Imelda Marcos* by Carmen Navarro Pedrosa, an Imelda supporter was quoted: 'If she likes something, whether it was chocolates, silk blouses, the finest leather bags or shoes, she would buy ten dozen, and when she was not sure whether she liked something, only five dozen.' Pedrosa also reported that during shopping sprees, 'Imelda would ransack department stores, floor by floor, section by section, with her party of courtiers and hangers-on in tow. It was not uncommon for her to run up bills of hundreds of thousands of dollars before she was through shopping at Harrods in London, Bloomingdale in New York, Takeshimaya in Tokyo, or at Liberty House in Honolulu.' Reacting to the description given her as a world class shopper, Imelda told *The Australian Magazine* in 1994 that 'yes, it is true I was a shopper, but I was shopping for the hospitals, museums, and housing projects. Because I could afford it I bought beautiful things – paintings, Matisse, Monet, works of art, for my country to fill the museums and the cultural centre. I wanted the best for my people. But for me personally, nothing'.

Imelda's portrait as shopper is indeed mythical. In fact, it was noted by a biographer that, while famous American screen luminaries Greta Garbo, Gloria Swanson and Paulette Goddard visited Florence to seek out the master of well-crafted shoes, Ferrugio and Leonardo of Salvatorre Ferragamo Shoes brought their shoes to Imelda's doorstep. According to Raymond Bonner, who wrote *Waltzing with a Dictator*, Imelda's 'spending binges are classic manifestation of the manic stage.' This information was given to him by the doctors who attended to Imelda during her psychiatric treatment in New York. Bonner claimed that Imelda was diagnosed as a manic-depressive and she was treated first with heavy tranquilisers and later with lithium.

Evita treated her clothes as an expression of her personality. She would order them unseen. Her clothes could seem loud or cheap, and for this she was much maligned. She still dressed, not as a politician, but as a film star. Rationalising her ways, Evita was quoted to have said: 'they [people] want to see me beautiful. Poor people don't want someone to protect them who are old and dowdy. They all have their dreams about me and I don't want to let them down.' The expensive jewels and clothes were her symbols as Evita, the president's wife, the benefactor of the poor, and the supporter of the union.

The popularity of the so-called Marcos jokes, particularly on Imelda, was also evident in the numerous jokes – unfunny and mildly obscene – that surfaced with Evita Peron as the subject. One joke said: When President and General Peron and his bejewelled wife Evita, who was really a tart, were before St. Peter during the time of judgment, General Peron stood up and steps on St. Peter's toe. St. Peter exclaims *puta* (whore) and Evita steps forward.

Evita's controversial European travel pales insignificantly compared to Imelda's countless travels abroad at government expense. During Evita's departure, the entire government and a substantial crowd gathered at the airport to see her take off in a specially equipped DC4 plane lent by the Spanish government. Another Spanish plane followed her, bearing the first lady's costumes and the group's luggage. To Imelda, ordering the country's flag carrier to take her to various points of the world was a standard operating procedure. Both women subscribed to the practice of giving people things. Whenever Evita met people whom she had known when she was an actress, her response was always the same: to give them presents. On one occasion, she gifted a former clothes designer, whom she found at 4am trying to start his old car, with an expensive new model of a convertible Packard. Evita was idolised not only because of her beauty and power but because of her habit of giving.

After the Marcoses fled Malacañang, a basement filled with both expensive and ordinary items was discovered. It was from this room that Imelda Marcos would send her assistant to retrieve gifts for her daily guests, particularly politicians. To Imelda, it was an investment that would become very handy during election time. The gift giving practice is tied up with the Filipino common trait of *utang na loob*.

In Argentina, the Peron and Peron team created the myth. He is the 'generous, good, hard-working, self-sacrificing, fatherly male, and she the incarnation of every feminine virtue, all love, humility and even more self-sacrifice'. Summing up the personality of Evita Peron, writer Fleur Cowles said: 'She was not a woman's woman with a warm remembrance of moments spent like any woman with her friends... not a man's woman either, even if she may once have been, but a woman *politico...* a woman too fabled, too capable, too sexless, too driven, too overbearing, too slick, too sly, too diamond-decked, too revengeful, too ambitious and far, far to under-rated far, far too long by our world.'

According to a CIA profile on Imelda Marcos and aptly titled *The Steel Butterfly*: 'Mrs. Marcos is ambitious and ruthless. Born a poor cousin of landed aristocracy, she has a thirst for wealth, power and public acclaim, and her boundless ego makes her easy prey for flatterers. Although she has little formal education, she is cunning.'

Evita Duerte de Peron is long gone, but the unsinkable Imelda Marcos is back and she is still playing the games she enjoys best – Philippine politics.

The Unsinkable Imelda Marcos

Wearing an expensive olive green dress with matching jewellery and with tears in her eyes, she congratulated her two lawyers and then shook their hands for a good job well done. Then looking a picture of triumph and victory, she faced reporters who had been waiting for the court announcement that day to hear her statement.

'I thank the Lord of relieving me of 32 cases that will subtract from the 901 cases filed by (former President Corazon) 'Cory' Aquino against the Marcoses.

'I do hope that this will subtract from the 901 cases while I am still alive so that I could fulfil my dream for my country and my people, for truth for the Marcoses would be justice for the Filipino.'

Madame Imelda Marcos, as how she likes to be addressed

these days, along with the deceased Roberto Benedicto and Hector Rivera, were accused of unlawfully opening 11 dollar accounts in Swiss banks under the names of 10 foundations linked to the Marcos family to hide alleged ill-gotten wealth. The 32 cases, the subject of the recent court ruling, covered a total $863 million found in Swss banks. In his decision,Judge Silvino Pampilo, Jr. of the Manila Regional Trial Court revealed that the *government failed to prove beyond reasonable doubt that the 78-year old widow of the late dictator Ferdinand Marcos* had stashed away $863 million in Swiss Bank accounts during the Marcos era.

Although part of the rich Romualdez clan, her branch of the family tree was the poorest. In fact, she had a poor, deprived and tragic childhood. She was the eldest of six children and has other five siblings by her father's first marriage. Imelda studied at the Holy Infant Academy, a convent school managed by Benedictine Sisters in Leyte. She later graduated with an education degree from the St. Paul's College. At an early age, she was aware of her plight as a poor relation to her more affluent Romualdez cousins. Despite poverty, she was thankful that she was born a Romualdez, she confided to her cousin years later in Manila. Her beauty and self-confidence was her passport to a better future and they brought her early successes. She became a beauty queen and received the title of the 'Rose of Tacloban'. Early on, she started to look at what provincial life would bring to her future.

An ambitious Imelda arrived in Manila in 1952, accompanied by her cousin Loreto Romualdez. She was determined to strive hard not only for herself but for her brothers and sisters too. She lived at another cousin's house in the city. Her first job was as a receptionist-salesgirl at the P.I. Domingo music store in Escolta. Her singing and piano skills helped her in her job. It was a new environment for her, different from the provincial life she left behind in Leyte. Imelda used the over-crowded jeepneys and buses to travel from her cousin's place to Escolta to work, like the rest of the many of her kind who flocked to the city from the province thinking to strike it rich. Although she was enjoying her work as a salesgirl, her father considered it demeaning for his eldest daughter, a Romualdez. Her politician cousin was forced to look for a 'decent' job for her. She became a clerk at the Central Bank.

At first, she entertained the idea that the name Romualdez alone would easily give her the break she needed to expand her contacts in the city, but it did not materialise. Determined as she was, she exploited her blood affinity with Daniel Romualdez, a well known politician, and at the same time decided to improve her chances by pursuing her voice lessons. She was enrolled at the College of Music and Fine Arts at the Philippine Women's University. Her voice teacher would recall later that she had a 'strong desire to be a success.' It was at this stage that the Miss Manila contest was announced. Imelda joined the beauty contest and clouded in controversy she was given a consolation title of *Muse of Manila*. As a beauty title holder, she was invited to model at fashion shows, and other charities. It was the exposure that she was waiting for.

In 1954, she met Ferdinand Marcos, a young ambitious and brilliant trial lawyer from the Ilocos province. He was then starting to make a name for himself in the city. Like Imelda, he grew up in the province. Marcos proposed marriage to Imelda at their first meeting. It was followed by an eleven day courtship. Many said that it was a perfect union between a beautiful, talented woman and a hard working, brilliant man.

Carmen Pedrosa in her book *The Untold Story of Imelda Marcos,* which was banned in the Philippines during the Marcos regime, said about the couple: 'Like Marcos, she entered the marriage with cold calculations. Beneath the idyllic romance lurked two wounded figures from the past, both driven by the will to win power and acceptance.'

The transformation of Imelda was fast, although initiation into a fulltime role of a politician's wife was not an easy one, but she adjusted to the new role very well. Imelda's lack of sophistication was supplanted by an image associated with the aristocratic and powerful Romualdez family which she exploited to the fullest. From a congressman representing his province, the ambitious Marcos became a senator. The demanding role of Imelda was expanding too. Reinventing herself follows her husband's rise to political power. Imelda claimed in an interview that she read a 'lot of books on Asia, communism, and just about everything else.' Her penchant for extravagance commenced at this stage. Her jewellery collection started to attract attention and became the topic of idle talk. Her jewels, expensive china and silver, are being passed on as family heirlooms of the rich Romualdez clan.

In 1965, Imelda Marcos worked hard for her husband's nomination as a presidential candidate. In fact, she became the 'secret weapon' of her husband during the campaign to nominate him. Many observed that she was a perfect political partner to an ambitious politician. Her motivation was very strong and unwavering. The partnership, which later became known as the 'conjugal dictatorship', was making a headway. Marcos concentrated on his political strategies while Imelda added the human touch. She was once quoted as describing the partnership as 'when Marcos was east, I was west, when Marcos was south, I was north.'

As the new chief executive of the Philippines, Marcos worked closely with his First Lady who now became his strong political ally. Imelda was determined. In one of her early pronouncements, she declared that she should project a different image of a First Lady, one who would not be remembered as a decorative appendage of the President. She would become a doer, accomplish things, and emphasised that her activities would complement Marcos government program. With her position secured, came the benefits. Her personal wealth in 1973 was placed at $250 million and this rose to $350 million three years later. After two decades, biographer Pedrosa estimated that Mrs. Marcos was worth $1.5 billion. In fact, Imelda was listed in 1975 by the *Cosmopolitan* as one of the ten riches women in the world, in the company of Elizabeth II of England, Dina Merrill, Christina Onassis, Barbara Hutton, Juliana of the Netherlands, and Begum Aga Kahan, Doris Duke, Madeleine Dassault, and the Duches of Alba. She had arrived, and the 'Rose of Tacloban' became part of an exclusive international circle of wealthy women.

According to the book *The Rise and Fall of Imelda Marcos* she was 'on top of the world' by 1980. She was a permanent resident at the $1,700 a day Royal Suite on the 37th floor of the Waldorf Towers whenever she was in New York. It was the same suite that was decorated and prepared for the use of Queen Elizabeth II of England in 1957. In spite of this change in economic status, she was never accepted by the 'oligarchs', the real rich people of the Philippines. During the expensive and lavish wedding reception for her youngest daughter Irene with Greggy Araneta, it was evident that, although the 'oligarchs' toasted the newlyweds with Dom Perignon, they were not taken in by the show of Marcoses' acquired wealth.

By the middle of the 1970s, observers noted that Imelda began to feel almost like real royalty. In fact, she was compared to King Ludwig II of Bavaria, the European monarch noted for the construction of stone monuments. Imelda had acquired an 'edifice complex.' She was obsessed with creating her own monuments in stone. Observers believed that this was her way of erasing the trauma created by her tragic childhood when she and her sisters and brothers lived in a garage, not in the big house where her other siblings lived comfortably. She was rewriting her past. The sprawling Cultural Center of the Philippines (CCP) complex situated at a reclaimed area in Manila is now a legacy of this intense passion. The CCP complex consisted of: the Philippine International Convention Centre, with a seating capaticy of 94,000, and at one time considered to be the largest conference centre in Asia; the 10,000 capacity Folk Arts Theatre, an arena-type theatre built in a record 77 days; the Tourist Pavillion, a fast food centre; the Philcite Trade Show Centre; the six-storey Film Palace, where many Filipino workers died and were buried during its construction; the elegant Coconut Palace; and the Philippine Plaza, a five-star hotel with a unique indoor waterfall. The CCP complex became the symbol of the Marcoses' version of the mythical kingdom of *Maharlika* where *Malakas* (strong), personified by Marcos and *Maganda* (beautiful) represented by Imelda, reign. It was the Filipino counterpart of the 'Acropolis'. Imelda was also behind the *Nayong Pilipino*, a miniature village representing various regions of the country, now gone but will resurface in the reclaimed area along the Diosdado Macapagal Highway. It was influenced by a similar village she visited in Europe. It was an expensive exercise.

As patroness of the arts and culture, Imelda pushed for the establishment of cultural sites within the proximity of the Complex. An archaeological relics and arts museum was established in Sta. Ana; it was followed by the Museum of Philippine Art located next door to the US Embassy. The Manila Metropolitan Museum, exclusively for foreign art, also opened at the restored fortification inside the Central Bank compound. To serve the interest of the artists, she caused the construction of the National Arts Centre in Laguna. Imelda was a dreamer. She fantasised and had grandiose ideas, a former employee of the Technology Resource Centre said. She projected a dubious impression, interpreted as endearing, adorable, child-like, but she was an achiever and a calculating woman.

During the announcement of her acquittal, she was still singing the same tune and said 'I do hope that this will subtract from the 901 cases while I am still alive so that I could fulfil my dream for my country and my people, for truth for the Marcoses would be justice for the Filipino.' This is similar to her statement many years ago that 'she offers herself to the Filipino people to mother the poor, the sick, the helpless and the young.'

In a published article, former American Ambassador to the Philippines, William Sullivan, described his relationship with Imelda Marcos during his term in Manila as a 'rocky one'. He described Imelda 'as an interesting woman, with a shrewd intelligence, a certain physical charm, an earthy sense of humour, but limited education.' As a wise woman, Imelda knew her limitations. Knowing the demand of her role in the international scene, she surrounded herself with staff of young 'experts' who briefed her about the subject expected to come up in her world travels. Ambassador Sullivan also described her as 'a quick study and could absorb information rapidly, giving her the appearance of being informed on nearly everything.'

Most recently, she voiced out her idea on how to handle the Philippine economy. The situation in the Philippines, according to her, should be measured 'not by economic indices but by the smiles and happiness of the people.' Imelda could not understand her critics. In answer to a question by an American journalist, she said: 'I'm a point of envy for some people... I'm too relaxed, too happy, too fulfilled.' In another interview, she exclaimed 'I am beyond logic and rationality'. Her shopping spree was legendary, from paying $2,000 for chocolates for her ward, Aimee, to the Idol's Eye diamond for which, according to reports, she paid $5.5 million dollars to a Chicago gem dealer. People the world over are mesmerised by her lifestyle.

The Marcos conjugal dictatorship ended in 1986 when President Marcos was ousted in a people power revolution that catapulted Mrs. Corazon Aquino, the widow of Senator Benigno Aquino, to the presidency. Marcos died in exile in Hawaii in 1989. Imelda's effort to return to the Philippines, after 'years of forced exile', was initially a frustration. It was an uphill battle against the Philippine government. For one, she was accused, with her late husband, of stealing $6.5 billion from the State and her notoriety for extravagance, particularly for shoes, did not fail to attract negative reactions.

Imelda Marcos was allowed to return to the Philippines in November 1991 and was greeted by ecstatic crowds of supporters. The Marcos loyalists were overjoyed. The former First Lady Imelda Marcos' life is full of drama. A year after her return, she ran in the presidential election. Announcing her decision to run for the presidency, she declared 'after months of direct consultation with our poor and oppressed citizens, I have decided to run for office to seek the presidency.' She got a respectable 10.3% of the vote. She was the seventh among the candidates who ran for the highest post of the land. During the 1995 election, she campaigned as representative of Leyte, while her son ran for senator. She was received like a queen as she moved from one isolated small barrio to another. Explaining her and her son's popularity, she said 'the people know the Marcoses have been victims of a conspiracy and are demanding us back.'

Like the famous Evita Peron of Argentina, Imelda Marcos remains popular, particularly among the poor, notwithstanding the belief that she is guilty of all the accusations filed against her. In fact, she was convicted of graft by a Philippine court in 1993 and sentenced up to 24 years imprisonment. She is free on bail while her appeal could take years. When she appears in public, a crowd almost always gathers, and wherever she goes there is spontaneous applause from the adoring public. Women, in particular, touch her, grab her hands, and kiss her cheek. She is practically mauled gently by her admirers and supporters. There was a last minute decision of the Commission on Election to prevent her from campaigning to represent Leyte province on a technicality for lack of residency. However, the people of Leyte voted her as their representative by nearly two-to-one against her political opponent. Nonetheless, she proclaimed herself winner of the election, even though she was disqualified from the polls. The Supreme Court came to her rescue and ruled by eight votes to five that she could take her seat in the House of Representatives despite objections from the Commission on Elections over the residency issue.

Explaining her mother's popularity, Ferdinand 'Bongbong' Marcos, Imelda's only son, who also served as representative of his father's province in 1992 but lost in the 1995 election when he ran for senator, said 'We have never been popular with the elite... but the people whose lives depended on my mother and father, they still remember us with affection and that's what counts'. He underscored his mother's accomplishments. 'My mother's social work was quite extensive and she had some very good projects and people remember that. What I always say is that people would not, after so many years and all that has been said, hold on to her memory with such affection unless their lives were actually affected in a good way. I find it remarkable and quite touching', he added.

In a 1996 interview, Imelda commented: 'there is nothing I

would not do for my country… they can take my money but not my good name, my dignity and my sacred honour. In all of this, if I have been strong it is the strength of someone who is at peace with the truth. I have a very childlike attitude to life. My only mistake was to look on everyone as good. At least I did my share of goodness. The Marcoses succeed because we give people hope', she concluded. Prior to her return to the Philippines after the Federal Jury in New York acquitted her of racketeering charges, Imelda told a visitor who saw her at the luxurious hotel: 'History is not through with me yet', an auspicious statement that surely guided her in her determination to bounce back and stay for good. Indeed, this is a triumph for a woman who was the most maligned person in the Philippines. Imelda seemed to be coming back at that time with a vengeance. With the recent court victory, she is confident of similar victory with her family's fight in the court against taipan Lucio Tan, one of the richest men in the Philippines. Madame Marcos and her son, Ilocos Norte Representative Ferdinand 'Bongbong' Marcos, insist that a bigger part of Tan's assets was owned by them and the late dictator Ferdinand Marcos only entrusted them to Tan, being a close ally and a business associate.

The court identified six corporations of Tan that have Marcos shares: Foremost Farms, Silangan Holdings Inc., Asia Brewery, Fortune Tobacco, Himmel Industries and Granspan Development Corporation. It is interesting to watch this next episode of the Marcos family saga headed by Madame Marcos and whether, like in other court cases where she was acquitted, she and the Marcos family will win the case against Tan, plus the remaining 10 cases out of the 901 cases filed against the Marcoses in the early 1990s still waiting to be decided. It appears that Madame Marcos will be in the limelight for many, many years to come. As if giving the public a preview of what will happen to the lawsuits against the Marcos family, Presidential Commission on Good Government (PCGG) Commissioner for Litigation, Narciso Nario, admitted in a recent interview that the outcome of the cases against the Marcos family will all depend on the evidence government prosecutors present to prove that guilt is beyond reasonable doubt. 'In many of the cases, the reason why we encountered defeat is probably because of our evidence, because the evidence available to us are mostly photocopies of the original documents'. He added, 'Under the law, if you present photocopies, these are inadmissible as evidence in court.' This seems to be what happened in the recent court decision that resulted in the acquittal of Imelda Marcos. The government could not prove beyond reasonable doubt that the 32 bank transfers to foreign accounts in Switzerland between 1968 and 1976 were undertaken by the former President Ferdinand Marcos, his wife and Benedicto. The court found that the prosecution failed to prove its charge of conspiracy among the accused and was unable to present witnesses who could give relevant testimonies to the case.

In other words, the case failed, in favour of Imelda Marcos due to lack of documentary proof. No wonder the Marcoses are in a fighting mood these days and brazen enough to claim in a recent hearing for a court case of ill-gotten wealth against Lucio Tan that a majority of the shares in Tan's six corporations belong to the late dictator. Just recently, Congressman Ferdinand 'Bongbong' Marcos suggested to the government, through the media, to drop all the cases against his family because for several decades now, the government could not prove its accusation against the Marcoses.

Select Bibliography

Primary Sources

British Parliamentary Papers, 1863-1864, 1880-1915.
CRS 26, Letters Received, 1894, SSC.
Commonwealth Act No. 602, 19 August 1940, Historical Data Bank, NHI, Philippines.
Commonwealth Act No. 731, 3 July 1946, Historical Data Bank, NHI, Philippines.
Country Education Profiles – The Philippines, National Office of Overseas Skills Recognition, Department of Employment, Education and Training, Canberra: AGPS, 1995.
Executive Order No. 23, Manila: Office of the President, 25 March 1936, Historical Data Bank, NHI, Philippines.
Executive Order No. 310, Manila: Office of the President, 4 December 1940, Historical Data Bank, NHI, Philippines.
J. Douglas, *Asiatic Aliens in Torres Strait*, 13 July 1895, PRE/102 8767/ 1895 (top Number 611/1896), Queensland State Archives.
Letter of H. Bowden to John Douglas, dated 30 December 1889, COL/ 75 (a) 1890/622, Queensland State Archives.
Marriage Register No. 002144, *Consolidated Index Master Report*, 1900-1904, Queensland Registrar-General's Office.
Memorandum Circular No. 34, Manila: Office of the President, 10 September 1986, Historical Data Bank, NHI, Philippines
'Memorandum of J. E. Mackey', Minister of Lands, Department of Lands and Survey, *Immigration and Advertising Australia*, dated 28 February 1908, Papers Presented to Parliament, Vol II, 1907-1908.
Naturalisation Certificate No. 16125, Z2210, SCT/CF27. 1899, 78, Queensland State Archives.
Newcastle US Consulate General Dispatch No.4, dated 16 June 1898. A photocopy of the document is in the author's library.
Presidential Decree No. 1413, 9 June 1978, Manila: Office of the President, Historical Data Bank, NHI Philippines.

Public Act No. 1365, Manila: Philippine Commission, 3 July 1905, Historical Data Bank, NHI, Philippines

Public Act No. 4258, Manila: Philippine Legislature, 1935, 6 November 1935, Historical Data Bank, NHI, Philippines.

'Report of the Royal Commission appointed to Inquire into the working of the Pearshell and Bêche-de-Mer Industries' (The Mackay Report), *QVP*, Brisbane: Acting Government Printer, 1908

'Report of the Commission appointed to inquire into the general working of the Laws regulating the Pearl-Shell and Bêche-de-Mer Fisheries in the Colony' (Hamilton Report), *QVP* Vol 2, Brisbane: Government Printer, 1897.

'Reports of the Government Resident at Thursday Island', *1880-1900*, Brisbane: Government Printer.

'Royal Decree Granting a Coat of Arms to the City of Manila', *Historical Bulletin*, Manila: Philippine Historical Association, Vol. xv, Nos. 1-4, 1971.

'Rules for the observance of the duties of neutrality during the state of war between Spain and the United States of America', British Foreign Office, Rule 3, Enclosure 2, C.A. 42-1898.

Statistical Report No. 2 (Settler Arrivals, 1988-1989), Canberra, AGPS, 1990.

Allan, Ian, Unpublished manuscript, *Newcastle 1898 – Probable base for Filipino Rebel Agent*, 1967,

Periodicals and Magazines

Archipelago, 1975
The Australian, 1990-1994
The Argus, 1898-1915
The Brisbane Courier, 1880-1899
The Fookien Times Yearbook, 1984-1985
The Good Weekend, magazine of the *Sydney Morning Herald*, 1995
The New Philippines, 1974
The Newcastle Morning Herald and Miners' Advocate, 1880-1915
Northern Territory Times and Gazette, 1890-1915
The Philippine Community Herald Newspaper, 1993-1994
The Queenslander, 1896-1899
The Sun-Herald, 1990-1994
The Sunday Telegraph, 1992-1994
The Sunday Times, 1890-1900

Select Bibliography

The Sydney Mail, 1880-1915
The Sydney Morning Herald, 1880-1915 and 1993-1994
Time (Summer) 1970
Torres Strait Pilot, 1880-1910

Books and Articles

Abella, Domingo, *The Flag of Our Fathers*, Manila: Milagros
    Romualdez-Abella, 1977.
—————, 'Introduction', *Catálogo Alfabético de Apellidos*,
    National Archives Publication No. D-3, Manila: Philippine
    National Archives, 1973.
—————, *From Indio to Filipino*, Manila: Milagros
    Romualdez-Abella, 1978.
Abbot, C. L. *Australia's Frontier Province*, Sydney: Angus and
    Robertson, 1950.
Agoncillo, Marcela M., *Reminiscences of the Agoncillo Family*, Manila:
    The Felipe Agoncillo and Marcela Mariño de Agoncillo Founda-
    tion, Inc., 1981.
Agoncillo, Teodoro A., *Malolos: The Crisis of the Republic*, Quezon
    City: University of the Philippines Press, 1960.
—————, *A Short History of the Philippines*, New York:
    Mentor Books, 1969.
—————, and Milagros C. Guerrero, *History of the Filipino
    People*, Quezon City: R. P. Garcia Publishing Company,
    1986.
Aguinaldo, Emilio, 'True Account of the Philippine Revolution',
    Historical Bulletin, Manila: Philippine Historical Association,
    1969.
Alger, Russell A., *The Spanish-American War*, New York: Harper's,
    1901.
Alzona, Encarnacion, 'Jose Rizal: A Biographical Sketch', *Internation-
    al Congress on Rizal*, Manila: Jose Rizal National Centennial
    Commission, 1961.
Ancheta, Herminia M. and Michaela B. Gonzalez, *Filipino Women in
    Nation Building*, Quezon City: Phoenix Publishing House, Inc., 1984.
Atkinson, Anne, *comp., Asian Immigrants to Western Australia*,
    Nedlands, Western Australia: University of Western Australia
    Press, 1988.

Bach, J., 'The Political Economy of Pearl Shelling', *The Economic History Review*, Vol. XIV, Nos. 1, 1 & 3, 1961 & 1962.

Bain, David Haward, *Sitting in Darkness: Americans in the Philippines*, Boston: Houghton Mifflin Company, 1984.

Barwick, Sir Garfield, 'Ourselves and Our Neighours', *Living with Asia*, Sydney: The Australian Institute of International Affairs, NSW Branch, 1963.

Battersby, Paul, 'Influential Circles: The Philippines in Australian Trade and Tourism', *Discovering Australasia*, Townsville, James Cook University Press, 1993.

Beaumont, J., ed., *Where to Now? Australia's Identity in the Nineties*, Sydney: Federation Press, 1993.

Birch, Alan and J. F. Blaxland, 'The Historical Background', *South Pacific Enterprise: The Colonial Sugar Refining Company Limited*, Sydney: Angus and Robertson, 1956.

Birrell, Robert, *The Chains that Bind: Family Reunion Migration to Australia in the 1980s.*, Canberra: AGPS, 1990.

Blount, James H., *American Occupation of the Philippines: 1898-1912.* Metro Manila, Philippines: Solar Publishing Corproation, 1968.

Boyce, William, D., *The Philippine Islands Illustrated*, New York: Rand McNally & Co., 1914.

Broinowski, Alison, *About Face: Asian accounts of Australia*, Melbourne: Scribe Publications, 2003.

Bruce, W. R. and T. Van der Veen, *Portrait of Asia*, Victoria: Whitcome & Tombs Pty. Ltd., 1970.

Burchill, Elizabeth, *Thursday Island Nurse*, Sydney: Rigby, 1972.

Burney, James, *A Chronological History of the Discoveries in the South Sea and Pacific Oceans*, 5 Volumes, London: Luke Hansard, 1803-1917

Che Man, W. K. , *Muslim Separatism: The Moros of Southern Philippines and the Malays of Southern Thailand*, Singapore: Oxford University Press, 1990.

Cook, James, *The Voyages of Captain James Cook round the world: Comprehending a history of the South Sea Islands, etc.,*London: Jacques and Wright, 1825.

Coles, Manuel A., 'International Recognition', *Pamana 32*, Manila: Cultural Centre of the Philippines, June 1978.

Collingridge, George, *The Discovery of Australia*, Sydney: F. Cunningham & Co., 1895.

Corpuz, O. D., 'Keynote Speech', *Proceedings of the Symposium on the Western Presence in South-East Asia*, Manila: National Historical Institute, 1982.

Select Bibliography

_____, *The Roots of the Filipino Nation*, Vols. 1 & 2, Quezon City: Aklahi Foundation, Inc., 1989.

_____, *The Philippines*, New Jersey: Prentice-Hall, Inc., 1965.

Cortes, Rosario Mendoza, *Pangasinan, 1572-1800*, Quezon City: University of the Philippines Press, 1974.

Crowley, Frank K., *A Documentary History of Australia: Colonial Australia, 1875-1900*, Vol. 3, West Melbourne: Nelson, 1978-1980.

_____, *Modern Australia in Documents, 1903-1939*, Melbourne: Wren, 1973.

Davis, Leonard, *The Philippines, People, Poverty and Politics*, London: Macmillan Press, 1987.

Day, David, *Smugglers and Sailors: Customs History of Australia 1788-1901*, Canberra: AGPS, 1993.

de Jesus, Edilberto, Jr., 'Aguinaldo and the American Consuls', *Philippine Historical Review*, Vol. 1, No. 2, Manila: International Association of Historians of Asia, 1966.

de la Costa, Horacio, S. J., *Readings in Philippine History*, Manila: Bookmark, Inc., 1965.

de los Santos, Epifanio, *The Revolutionists: Aguinaldo, Bonifacio and Jacinto*, Manila: National Historical Institute, 1973.

de Man, J., *Recollection of a Voyage to the Philippines*, translation by E. Aguilar Cruz from the 1875 French edition, Manila: National Historical Institute, 1984.

De Ocampo, Esteban A., *The First Filipino Diplomat – Felipe Agoncillo*, Manila: National Historical Institute, 1977.

Del Pilar, Marcelo H., *Frailocracy in the Philippines*, translation from Spanish by Leonor Agrava, Manila: National Historical Institute, 1979.

Deutsch, Karl W., 'The Growth of Nations: Some Recurrent Patterns of Political and Social Integration', *Southeast Asia – The Politics of National Integration*, ed. John T. McAlister, Jr., New York, Stanford University: Random House, 1973.

Dewey, George, *Autobiography of George Dewey, Admiral of the Navy*, New York: Scribner's, 1913.

Douglas, John, 'Asia and Australasia', *The Nineteenth Century and After*, Vol. 52, July-December 1902.

Edwardes, Michael, *The West in Asia, 1850-1914*, London: BT Batsford Ltd., 1967.

Elliot, Charles Bourke, *The Philippines to the end of the Commission Government: A Study in Tropical Democracy,* New York: Greenwood Press, 1968, a reprint of the 1917 edition.

Eminent Filipinos, Manila: National Historical Commission, 1965.

Escalante, Rene R., *The Bearer of Americana: The Philippine C areer of William H. Taft, 1900-1903*, Quezon City: New Day Publishers, 2007.

Farwell, George, *Mask of Asia – The Philippines*, Sydney: F. W. Cheshire, 1966.

Fernandez, Leandro H., *The Philippine Republic*, New York: Colombia University, 1926.

Fernandez, Rodolfo, 'The Terno: How it turned Filipino', *Pamana 32*, Manila: Cultural Centre of the Philippines, June 1978.

Fermin, Jose D., *1904 World's Fair: The Filipino Experience*, Diliman, Quezon City: The University of the Philippines Press, 2004.

Fisk, E. K., *Policy Options in the Torres Strait*, Vol. 4, Canberra: AGPS, 1975.

Fitzgerald, Shirley, *Sydney 1842-1992*, Sydney: Hale & Iremonger, 1992.

Foreman, John, *The Philippine Islands*, New York: Charles Scribner's Sons, 1906.

Gamboa, Melquiades J., *Elements of Diplomatic and Consular Practice, A Glossary*, Quezon City: Central Law Book Publishing Co., Inc. 1966.

Goldsworthy, David, Ed., *Facing North: A Century of Australian engagement with Asia*, Vol. 1, Melbourne: Melbourne University Press, 2001.

Goodwin, C. D. W., *The Image of Australia – British Perception of the Australian Economy from the 18th to the 20th Century*, Durham, N.C.: Duke University Press, 1974.

Greenwood, G. ed. *Australia – A Social and Political History*, Sydney: Angus and Robertson, 1974.

_____, and C. Crimshaw, *ed. Documents on Australian International Affairs, 1901-1918*, West Melbourne: Thomas Nelson (Australia), 1977.

Guevara, Sulpicio, *The Laws of the First Philippine Republic (Laws of Malolos, 1898-1899)*, Manila: National Historical Commission, 1972.

Hakluyt, Richard, *The Principal Navigations, Voyages, Traffiques and Discoveries of the English Nation*, London: Dent, 1927-1928.

Heine-Geldern, Robert, 'Conceptions of State and Kingship in Southeast Asia', *Southeast Asia, the Politics of National Integration*, ed., John T. McAlister, Jr., New York, Stanford University: Random House, 1973.

Hernandez, Jose M., *et. al, Rizal's Life and His Works*, Quezon City: Bustamante Press, 1972.

Historical Calendar, Manila: National Historical Commission, 1970.

Idries, Ion, *Forty Fathoms Deep – Pearl Divers and Sea Rovers in Australian Seas*, Sydney: Angus and Robertson, 1937.

Ileto, Reynaldo C., 'Philippine-Australian Interactions in the late Nineteenth Century', *Discovering Australasia*, Townsville: James Cook University, 1993.

Jackson, Richard T., 'Recent Migration to Australia from the Philippines', *Discovering Australasia*, Townsville: James Cook University, 1993.

Kalaw, Maximo M., *Philippine Government, its Development, Organisation and Activities*, Manila: Maximo M. Kalaw, 1948.

Kalaw, Teodoro M., *The Philippine Revolution*, Mandaluyong, Rizal: Jorge B. Vargas Filipiniana Foundation, 1969.

_____, ed. *Epistolario Rizalino*, Vol. V, Part 2, Manila: National Library of the Philippines, 1938.

Kasaysayan - History of the Filipinos, Manila: National Historical Commission, 1970.

Langdon, Robert, 'Spanish Navigators in the Pacific', *Some Historical Ties between Australia and the Spanish World*, Sydney: Spanish Cultural Society, 1988.

Lardizabal, Amparo S., 'The Filipino Woman', *Women of Distinction*, Manila: *Bukang Liwayway*, 1967.

Licuanan, Verginia Benitez, *Filipinos and Americans: A Love–Hate Relationship*, Manila: Baguio Country Club, 1982.

Legarda, Benito J., *After the Galleons*, Quezon City: Ateneo de Manila University Press, 1999.

Le Gentil, Guillaume Joseph Hyacinthe Jean Baptiste de la Galaisiere, *A Voyage to the Indian Seas*, Manila: Filipiniana Book Guild, 1964 reprint.

MacMicking, Robert, *Recollections of Manila and the Philippines during 1848, 1849 and 1850*, Manila: Filipiniana Book Guild, 1967, Reprint of the original London 1851 edition.

Malcolm, George A., *First Malayan Republic: The Story of the Philippines*, Boston, USA: The Christopher Publishing House, 1951.

Mallat, J., *The Philippines, History, Geography, Customs, Agriculture, Industry and Commerce of the Spanish Colonies in Oceania*, English translation by Pura S. Castrence from the original 1846 French edition, Manila: National Historical Institute, 1983.

Mangiafico, Luciano, *Contemporary American Immigrants, Patterns of Filipino, Korean and Chinese Settlements in the United States*, New York: Praeger, 1988.

Mayers, Marvin K., *A Look at Filipino Lifestyles*, Dallas, Texas: Sil Museum of Anthropology, 1980.

Miller, Stuart Creighton, *Benevolent Assimilation: The American Conquest of the Philippines, 1899-1903*. New Haven: Yale University Press, 1982.

National Committee on Museums and Galleries, *A Guidebook to the Museums of Metro Manila*, Manila: Sub-Commission on Cultural Heritage, Presidential Commission on Culture and Arts, 1988.

National Library of the Philippines, *A Britisher in the Philippines (Letters of Nicholas Loney)*, Manila: National Library, 1964.

Nelson, Raymond, *The Philippines*, New York: Walker and Company, 1968.

Ocampo, Galo, 'Symbols of the Nation', *Symbols of the State*, Quezon City: Bureau of Local Government, Department of Local Government and Community Development, 1975.

Osborne, Milton, *Southeast Asia: An Introductory History*, Sydney: George Allen & Unwin, 1979.

O'Toole, G. J. A., *The Spanish War: An American Epic – 1898*, New York: Norton, 1984.

Perdon, Renato, 'The Preservation of Traditional Culture for National Identity in the Philippines', *Problems and Issues in Cultural Heritage Conservation*, Honolulu, Hawaii, 1985.

_____, 'The Ethnic Ensemble', *Haylaya, : Celebration After Spiritual Renewal*, Metro Manila: The Presidential Commission for the Rehabilitation and Development of Southern Philippines, 1980.

_____, *Brown Americans of Asia*, Sydney: The Manila Prints, 1998.

Phelan, John Leddy, *The Hispanisation of the Philippines*, London: The University of Wisconsin Press, 1967.

Pomeroy, William, *American Neo-Colonialism: Its Emergence in the Philippines and Asia*, New York: International Publishers, 1970.

Relaga-Santos, Henrie, 'My Dad Said, 'No'', *Shaking the Family Tree*, Pasig City: Anvil Publishing, Inc., 1998.

Quiason, Serafin D., *et.al.*, *Kasaysayan ng Asya*, Manila: Phoenix Publishing Co., 1990.

Quintos, Rolando N., 'Mabini and Nationalism,' *Lectures on Great Filipinos and others, 1967-1970*, Manila: National Historical Institute, 1971.

Select Bibliography

Quirino, Carlos, *Under Four Flags*, Bristol, England: J. W. Arrowsmith Ltd., 1970.

Resurreccion, Celedonio O., 'Why we should change the name Philippines?', *Historical Bulletin*, Manila: Philippine Historical Association, Vol. XI, No. 2, 1967.

Robles, E. G., *The Philippines in the Nineteenth Century*, Quezon City: University of the Philippines Press, 1969.

Romulo, Carlos P., *The Asian Mystique*, Manila: Solidaridad Publishing House, 1970.

Salamanca, Bonifacio S., *The Filipino Reaction to American Rule, 1901-1913*, Quezon City: New Day Publishers, 1984.

Sta. Maria, Felice, Corazon S. Alvina and, *Halupi: Essays on Philippine Culture*, Quezon City: GCF Books, 1989.

Schumacher, John N., *The Propaganda Movement: 1880-1895*, Manila: Solidaridad Publishing House, 1973.

Shannon, Ian, *The Philippines: Australia's Neighbour, a Study in Development in South East Asia*, Canberra: Committee for Economic Development of Australia, 1965.

Sheridan, Richard Brinsley, *The Filipino Martyrs, A Story of the Crime of February 4, 1899*, London: John Lane, the Bodley Head, 1900.

Shnukal, Anna, GuyRamsay and Yuriko Nagata, Eds., *Navigating Boundaries: The Asian Diaspora in Torres Strait*, Canberra: Pandanus Books (ANU), 2004

The Symbols of the State, Quezon City: Bureau of Local Government, Department of Local Government and Community Development, 1973.

Tate, D. J. M., *The Making of Modern South-East Asia – The European Conquest*, New York: Oxford University Press, 1971.

Taylor, John R. M., *The Philippine Insurrection Against the United States*, Vols. 1-5, Pasay City: Eugenio Lopez Memorial Foundation, 1971.

Timberman, David G., *A Changeless Land: Continuity and Change in the Philippine Politics*, Singapore: Institute of Southeast Asian Studies, 1991.

Varma, R., *Australia and Southeast Asia: The Crystallisation of a Relationship*, New Delhi: Abhinav Publications, 1974.

Villa, S. A., 'The Flight and Wanderings of General Emilio Aguinaldo from Bayambang to Palanan, 1899-1901: A Diary', *Historical Bulletin*, Manila: Philippine Historical Association, 1969.

Von der Mehden, Fred R., *Religion and Nationalism in Southeast Asia*, London: The University of Wisconsin Press, 1968.

Walsh, E. John, *The Philippine Insurrection 1899-1902: America's Only try for an Overseas Empire,* New York: Franklin Watts, Inc., 1973

Welch, Richard E., Jr., *Response to Imperialism: The United States and the Philippine-American War, 1899-1902*, Chapel Hill, North Carolina Press, 1979.

Worcester, Dean, *The Philippine Past and Present*, 2nd ed., New York, 1914.

Younghusband, George John, *The Philippines and Round About*, Manila: National Historical Institute, 2004 reprint.

About the author:

The author was born and raised in the Philippines. He worked for the National Historical Institute of the Philippines for many years as historical researcher, then as archivist with the City of Sydney Archives, Australia, until his retirement in 2007. He has a Master of Arts in Asian Studies degree from the University of New South Wales and has published a number of books on Filipino history and language.

At present, he is an accredited NAATI translator and editor of the Filipino Section of *Bayanihan News,* a Filipino community newspaper in Australia. His other books include:

Sydney Aldermen: A Biographical Register of Sydney Aldermen, 1843-1992 (1995)
Brown Americans of Asia (1998)
Pocket Filipino Dictionary (2002)
Essential Filipino Phrase Book (2002)
Moving Out in Filipino (2003)
English-Filipino/Filipino-English Wordbook (2003)
Pocket English-Filipino-English Dictionary (2004)
Technical and Business English-Filipino Wordbook (2007)
Learning and Speaking Filipino (2008).